" *WHAT DO I SAY WHEN...* "

A Guidebook for Getting Your Way with People on the Job

Muriel Solomon

PRENTICE HALL
Englewood Cliffs, New Jersey 07632

Prentice-Hall International (UK) Limited, *London*
Prentice-Hall of Australia Pty. Limited, *Sydney*
Prentice-Hall Canada, Inc., *Toronto*
Prentice-Hall Hispanoamericana, S.A., *Mexico*
Prentice-Hall of India Private Limited, *New Delhi*
Prentice-Hall of Japan, Inc., *Tokyo*
Simon & Schuster Asia Pte. Ltd., *Singapore*
Editora Prentice-Hall do Brasil, Ltda., *Rio de Janiero*

10 9 8 7

Library of Congress Cataloging-in-Publication Data

Solomon, Muriel.
    What do I say when — : a guidebook for getting your way with
people on the job / by Muriel Solomon
        p. cm.
    Includes index.
    ISBN 0-13-955782-2
    1. Business communication.   2. Communication in personnel
management.   I. Title.
HF5718.S637 1988
658.4'52   88-21436
                                                            CIP

ISBN 0-13-955782-2

ISBN 0-13-951617-4 PBK

PRENTICE HALL
BUSINESS & PROFESSIONAL DIVISION
A division of Simon & Schuster
Englewood Cliffs, New Jersey 07632

Printed in the United States of America

*To my husband, Judge Harold Solomon,
for his unwavering encouragement while
generously sharing his wit and wisdom.*

Acknowledgments

Working in business, government, and with the media and civic organizations, I've had a multitude of bosses, colleagues, and staff. I'm most grateful to them for encouraging me to develop the practical and tactical communication strategies given in this book. Also, I deeply appreciate the guidance I received from Ellen Lohsen, my editor, for her patient and invaluable assistance in shaping this book.

How to Use This Guidebook

As the communications director for a large office, I spent much of my time each day coaching people on what to say to the people they worked with. People on every rung of the corporate ladder came to me for help with an assortment of communications problems. "What do I say when. . ." was their burning question. They wanted to know what words to use to ask for a raise, what to say to motivate a lazy worker, or what was the best way to handle anger at a co-worker.

To help coach these employees, I began looking for a practical, workable advice book for the office on what to say and how to say it better. I could find nothing like this in print. So, out of all my experiences, I decided to design a guidebook that fills this distinct gap.

"What Do I Say When. . ." is a collection of put-downs, put-overs and put-acrosses to help you say what's on your mind without putting your foot in your mouth. It is a straightforward, reliable reference that you can keep in your desk drawer to pick up when you need it. You'll find the exact words to use when you find yourself tongue-tied, imposed upon, or burning up.

The book is divided into three parts, covering dialogues to use with the people you work for, people you work with, and the people who work for you. Even though you may face the same problem with your boss and your secretary, you'll want tailor-made responses to cope with each person.

You'll find the most effective phrases to use to:

- ask for the raise you deserve
- sound confident when standing up to a bully
- voice a negative opinion
- snag attention during conversations and presentations
- light a fire under the dead wood in your department
- get others to toot your horn
- run a meeting or creative session

Communication in today's office is more important than ever—it can either make or break you. You can test your communication effectiveness by taking the quizzes at the beginning of each chapter. You'll learn what you're saying wrong—and how to say it right.

Whether your ambition is to stay put, move up or move out, you need the words to get you where you want to be. *What do I Say When. . ."* puts the words right in your mouth.

* * *

AUTHOR'S NOTE: In recent years, the role of women in business has expanded beyond the traditional assistant roles. It is not uncommon for women to supervise men as well as women. Therefore, I hope it will be understood that when I use the personal pronouns "he," "his," and "him" I am referring to women and men alike.

Contents

1. Assure good reception—don't be a telephone pest
2. Strategize before you dial
3. Call back even if you don't have the answer
4. Hang up gracefully—don't prolong the call
5. Use the phone when you haven't time to write

Four Techniques to Capture Attention with your
Voice / **176**

1. Practice daily voice drills
2. Scrutinize your expressions and mannerisms
3. Select the clearest and most appropriate word
4. Be explicit and decisive

PART THREE—WHAT TO SAY TO THE PEOPLE WHO WORK FOR YOU

PART ONE

What to Say to the People You Work For

CHAPTER 1

How to Communicate with a Difficult Boss

QUIZ #1. HOW WELL DO YOU HANDLE A DIFFICULT BOSS?

There are many types of "problem" bosses. If you find yourself in an office headed by one, what would you say in the following situations? An interpretation of your choices follows.

1. Whenever your bullying boss attacks your ego, you

    (a) say nothing to the boss, but complain to co-workers.
    (b) say nothing but plot ways to get revenge.
    (c) speak up, asking the boss treat you with respect.

2. Your pompous boss acts as though you're a servant to royalty. You

    (a) use flattery to meet the boss's hunger for recognition.
    (b) report the high-handed behavior to your boss's superior.
    (c) appeal to his desire to be regarded as a professional.

3. The boss keeps promising to get repairs done and never does. You

    (a) repeatedly say how much this inconveniences you.
    (b) increase your nagging to get the boss to do something.

3

(c) stress how neglect will negatively affect the boss.

4.   After your boss reluctantly gives you the additional responsibility you've been requesting, you

(a) double-check every move with the boss to assure accuracy.

(b) check with the boss after finishing the assignment.

(c) keep your boss informed with periodic progress reports.

5.   Your new boss was recently promoted from your job. Now you find the boss overly critical, and so you

(a) avoid speaking to him until things settle down.

(b) say, with frankness, "Boss, you're picking on me."

(c) ask the boss for advice, understanding your job is still "his baby."

6.   When your boss breaks the chain of command, bypassing you to directly instruct your subordinates, you

(a) appreciate the help although it decreases the respect you get.

(b) warn your subordinates to take orders only from you.

(c) point out to your boss the potential problems this causes.

7.   Your boss is quick, clever, confident, and conceited. When a problem needs his intervention, you report it,

(a) giving a series of alternatives at the end.

(b) ending with your suggestion for handling it.

(c) waiting until the boss requests alternatives.

8.   Your boss gets angry and frequently explodes abusively. You

(a) say nothing, ducking if the boss throws things.

(b) stand your ground, trying to outshout the boss.

(c) get away quickly if you fail to calm the exploder.

9.   Your boss delegates everything and has a laissez-faire style that makes you wonder if the boss cares about what's happening. You

    (a) say nothing, do your job, and hope to escape blame.

    (b) take over, reporting when the boss asks for information.

    (c) take over, keeping the boss continually informed.

10. You can't reason with your boss and you're unable to go over the boss's head to complain, so you

    (a) say nothing, hoping the boss will leave or transfer.

    (b) risk organizing complainants in order to have more weight.

    (c) write anonymous letters hoping the boss will pick up on it.

Interpretation

If your answers are mostly in group A, you have difficulty getting to the heart of the problem, you tend to take evasive action, or to seek reassurance, rather than trying to improve the situation. Working for a difficult boss, you feel helpless, unable to speak up.

If your answers are mostly in group B, you take risks sometimes unnecessarily. Your hard-hitting responses may give you momentary satisfaction but they rarely accomplish long-lasting results and might even worsen the situation.

If your answers are mostly in group C, you've probably been studying the boss's reactions and plan your strategy accordingly. You appeal to your supervisor's better instincts and desired outcomes, as well as what seems to be in the best interest of the company.

HOW TO TALK TO THE BOSS WHO'S MAKING YOU MISERABLE

It is unlikely that you can change your boss's behavior. Although you may be tempted to undermine your supervisor, this strategy will not be viewed favorably by the top management. Nevertheless, you need a strategy to survive the pangs of distress being inflicted upon you. Remaining passive only makes you take out your frustrations on colleagues, friends, and family. Whether you decide to stay or leave you can't afford to tell the ogre what you think.

Your boss may retaliate by preventing a promotion or raise. If you try to change jobs, a potential employer will check your references with your current boss.

Stuck with a problem boss, you have two choices: Try to change the situation in your office and, if that doesn't work, change your office. While most supervisors fall somewhere between a pain and a paragon, watch your jabs and hope for the patience of Job when you have to deal with potentates, perfectionists, or prima donnas.

What to Say When Your Boss Is Too Bossy

This boss loves his title and delights in burying you beneath royal commands which he issues in an abusive, tyrannical, dictatorial, or argumentative fashion. How can you deflate his delusions of omnipotence and still keep your job?

Muzzling the boss who barks nonstop orders

Your boss makes you feel like a serf. He expects you to cower under his absolute power. Working under the tension of screaming mandates and belittling criticism, you and your colleagues make unnecessary mistakes which consequently lower productivity.

TIP: Calmly, and without threatening your manager's self image, tell him about the feelings you've been suppressing and why it's affecting the work.

Strategy Your objective is to stop the verbal abuse without getting fired. Let the boss know that indulging his right to rant is bad for business.

Nell told me her boss has devised a stack of orders supposed to carry out company objectives, but they really just reflect his whims. Nell's too scared to tell him that he's treating her like a slave. Don't get into a hassle, I advised her, but tell him why he makes you nervous or the bondage will continue ad infinitum.

What to say   The more he yells, the more Nell must stay calm and respectful of her boss's position.

> ***Nell:***   "Boss, I know how hard you're trying to increase production, but when you bark orders at me, I don't function as well. I wonder if we could work out something else."
>
> ***Boss:***   "What do you mean 'bark orders'? You know that's just the way I talk when I get excited. I have to let you know what's important."
>
> ***Nell:***   "That's right, boss. you do have to tell me what's important. But how about our agreeing in advance to some specific goals for increased production. Then we can. ...."

Once they started talking to each other, there was a change—a slow and gradual change. The boss finally realized that it's really futile to act like a potentate.

When your boss suddenly starts throwing his weight around

On the flip side is the barking boss who used to be a great supervisor—pleasant, nice to be with, always joking—then he suddenly starts throwing his weight around. In addition to office pressures, he's obviously having some personal problem.

> **TIP:**   As a united group, be supportive without prying or asking the boss to disclose his personal problem to subordinates. Your objective is to help the boss and the office return to normal.

Strategy   The team's showing concern will help the boss

(1) see the effect his worrying about the personal problem is having on the department

(2) realize he has to start coping with his problem (seeking professional help or whatever is needed).

No one can figure out why Steve began venting his anger on a good crew or what they were going to do about it. Everybody really liked Steve until he started throwing his weight around. He has a powerful position in the organization and it would be a mistake to try to go over his head. According to Regina, Steve's also been gaining weight. He's not doing his own work because he's so busy standing over his staff clobbering them with cruel and spiteful words. He demands the impossible, and claims they're doing everything wrong.

What to say   Singing the "I don't want him you can have him he's too fat for me" blues won't solve the problem. I suggested the group invite their boss to plop down for a diet soda to talk it over.

> ***Regina:***   "Steve, we realize that something is wrong and want to know how we can help you. We have the best unit because everyone works as a team. Just tell us what we can do for you."

By bolstering Steve, the team—and Steve—were able to get through this rough time. Knowing his department wanted to pull together, Steve exercised restraint and began to bend. Eventually his problem was resolved and Steve returned to his former pleasant self.

Slowing down the boss who wants something yesterday

Among the bossy bosses are the ones who run everyone ragged. Unrealistically anxious to succeed, they drive their staff, who are on the verge of collapse trying to keep up with the boss's perpetual motion.

> **TIP:**   Tell the boss to stop for a minute to let the group recoup. Politely remind him that even the best workers need a break.

Strategy   Your objective is to regulate the pace without incurring the boss's wrath. Enlist the entire staff to apply gentle, good natured pressure, and ask the boss to lighten up.

The office just finished a successful but exhausting three-week effort and the very next morning Liz was on the phone with a hundred things to be done on the next project. Without giving her people time to reflect, evaluate, or get a second wind, Liz was once again pushing everyone too hard.

What to say   Gerri wanted to know what they could say without angering Liz. We decided the best way to enlighten her was with a little cheerful teasing. The whole group joined in after Gerri began.

> **Gerri:**   "Liz, please slow down. We'd have to be made of iron, or taking daily doses of it, to brace for your pace."

After hearing from Gerri and other staff members, Liz stopped pushing—temporarily. From time to time they had to repeat this method to get her to unwind.

When your boss is grinding you into the ground

You wake up in the middle of the night in a cold sweat. You can't figure out what's happened, much less what lies ahead. While you suffer silently, it's easy for your tyrannical boss to grind you into the ground, escalating personal attacks and humiliating you in front of others.

TIP: Before standing up to the tyrant, investigate the possibility of transferring, calling your network of friends, learning what's available and start formulating a back-up plan to move out.

Strategy   Your objective is to relieve the stress before you become too sick to work at all. Whatever the price (such as working somewhere else for lower pay) no job is worth unrelenting emotional torment.

Ever since her boss, Zack, was promoted to project director and Belle to project secretary, Zack started complaining about her work which he used to find perfectly acceptable. ("You call this a letter? My ten-year-old could do better!") At first Belle turned the other cheek, but you can't appease a provoker. ("I know I'm late again, Agnes. Belle has my schedule all screwed up—as usual. She can't get anything right.")

Because Zack has no legitimate basis for firing her, Belle concluded he was trying to force her to quit. Regardless of the reason for his abuse, Belle can't keep running to the restroom to regain her composure.

What to say   Until Belle could make other arrangements, she had to demand respect so that the remainder of her stay under the tyrant's rule would be tolerable. Summoning her nerve, she made an appointment for a few *uninterrupted* minutes of Zack's time. Belle practiced a short, memorized speech which she delivered calmly while looking Zack straight in the eye.

> ***Belle:***   "Zack, I understand you want things done your way, and you have every right to criticize my work. But nobody can give you the right to mortify me in front of the staff and to show utter contempt for my feelings. I want you to respect me as a fellow human being. I have requested a transfer and, until that comes through, there is no reason why we cannot be civil to each other."

Then she threw back her shoulders, stood erect, and walked slowly from Zack's office as he sat there dumbstruck. Zack didn't fire Belle. The tirades stopped. They will never be friends, but Zack did help her find another job. He even volunteered to write her a nice letter of recommendation.

What to Say When Your Boss Demands Perfection

Overzealous nit-pickers quote every company rule like it's a sacred law. They believe they are more competent than any of their peers and even their own boss. They believe their subordinates had better clear every minor decision through them. Perfectionists often complain they do all the work. Even if this were true, employees don't get spoiled all by themselves.

How to get your boss to delegate

Your boss solves everything himself and when anything goes wrong, he covers up the problem. He is, therefore, reluctant to delegate although you would like to be given more responsibility.

> **TIP:** To overcome your boss's resistance, whatever changes you suggest have to be tactful and gradual. You can build confidence by addressing the concerns you think the boss has, before he has a chance to tell them to you.

Strategy Your objective is to win your boss's trust and confidence so that he or she will be more willing to delegate. The strategy is two-fold:

(1) Be pleasantly persistent and reassuring, willing to prove yourself
(2) Appeal to the boss's desire for more time to do something else he doesn't have time for.

Ron is an Accounts Officer who wants more office responsibility and hopes to become a CPA. He unsuccessfully suggested taking over the payroll duties from his boss, Toby.

What to say To be more convincing this time, Ron anticipated and was ready for Toby's reaction.

> ***Ron:*** "Toby, I think I understand why you're hesitant to let me do the payroll. You're concerned that I'll keep running to you with 'What should I do about. . .?' And that would just add to your problems. I promise to learn where to find information or who to call and I won't bug you unless I'm really stuck. Giving me a chance will also free you to work on the new system."

With the added responsibility, Ron had to make new kinds of decisions. He wanted a chance to show he could handle it and now he has to handle it with minimal interruptions.

Telling your boss to get off your back—nicely

When you were hired your boss made it very clear what you were expected to do. Now you'd like to be free to do it. Your back-seat driver boss is driving you up the wall and you want to quit.

> **TIP:** Before speaking up to your boss, be certain that you have been sending him whatever type of progress reports you agreed upon and that you are getting your work out early enough to get maximum mileage from the effort.

Strategy   Your objective is to do your own work without your boss constantly checking up on you. Appeal to something the boss wants to convince him to back off.

Wendy is constantly monitoring each contact Milt makes along with every other detail of his work. Milt is ready to resign because he's convinced that he's giving a trouble-free performance and the real problem is having a boss managing from over his shoulder.

What to say   Milt agreed to talk it over with Wendy.

> **Milt:**   "Wendy, everyone appreciates your dedication and several of us would really be grateful to you if you'd give us the chance to earn your confidence. If you could let us work without constant checking and directing, you'll see our whole unit will come through for you and we'll soon be outdistancing all the other divisions."

By appealing to the boss's desire to have her division perform better than other divisions, Milt was able to convince Wendy to give them some breathing room.

Reasoning with the overcritical boss who used to have your job

Before being promoted, your boss had the job you now hold. Now he's criticizing your performance to others on the staff.

You're especially disappointed because you have tried to be considerate and not bother your boss while he was adjusting to his new position and you were getting familiar with yours.

> **TIP:** When your boss is having trouble letting go of his or her former job, start by acknowledging his or her expertise. Remember, it's a sign of wisdom, not weakness, to ask for advice.

Strategy   Your objective is to get your new boss to give you a chance to show what you can do. By severing ties to old positions, your boss won't have to prove to everybody that he or she is the only one who can handle your job.

Elliot was director of the transportation division before being promoted to head of the department. Murphy assumed Elliot's position as director and is feeling hurt and confused that his boss Elliot is complaining about him to their mutual friends. Why didn't Elliot come to Murphy first?

What to say   Elliot probably can't accept that someone else is the director of the division. Murphy has to show understanding for this concern.

Murphy: "Elliot, I know how much of yourself you've put into the project and that whatever comments you've made about my handling it was meant to keep the project up to your high standards. So I'd like to discuss some approaches with you and get your suggestions on the best way to proceed."

Elliot: "I've been waiting for you to come in."

Elliot thought Murphy owed him a courtesy call. And he did. Once Murphy broke the ice, they were able to discuss their differences.

When the boss does your job by instructing your staff

In a desire to have everything done exactly the way they want it, some bosses interfere with responsibilities they have delegated to their assistants—not because they are back-seat drivers, but because they truly want to be helpful. They don't realize that they are undermining your authority and making your supervisory tasks more difficult when they deal directly with your staff instead of going through you.

TIP: A missing link breaks the chain of command. Even though your boss is above you, don't let him go over your head.

Strategy Your objective is to stop the boss's interference without risking a confrontation. Go to the boss as a friend, gently pointing out how he would be damaged by the consequences of what you know the boss perceived to be a generous gesture.

When Gene had a problem, he bypassed his boss Vera and went directly to John, Vera's boss. John told Gene how to handle the problem, inadvertently going over Vera's head.

What to say Vera had to convince John to follow the established chain of command.

> **Vera:** "John, I know you have so much on your mind that you didn't realize you were opening a can of worms by helping Gene with his problem yesterday. I'm sure you were just concerned with giving him an answer that would let him get back to work.
>
> "However, if we continue to break the chain of command, you'll have a continuous parade of workers at your door with problems that can easily be solved at a lower level without taking up your valuable time. And an organizational set up that's been working well will fall apart."

John agreed that the chain of command exists because it's efficient and effective. Be sure to establish that it is to the boss's advantage to maintain the chain.

What to Say When Your Boss Gets Temperamental

Prima donna bosses are easily excitable. They scale emotions from glee to gloom while you're standing there wondering what triggered the mood swing. Whether they are quick and bright or pompous incompetents, you can't tune them out, but you can try to get on the same wavelength by singing the same song.

Approaching the boss who has it all figured out

Your boss is clever, confident, and conceited. She gets annoyed when a subordinate doesn't grasp something as fast as she does. Whatever is discussed, she's three steps ahead. She toys with her staff, asking for ideas and then, after rejecting all suggestions, tells how the issue should be resolved.

> **TIP:** Your objective is to earn your boss's respect. Come on strong, but not threatening. Give the facts, clearly acknowledging you know who is in charge. This type of boss usually wants to hear only the problem, not the solution, which she believes she can figure out better than anyone else.

Strategy Pick up your pace. Be prepared with ideas but don't offer them until requested.

(1) For short term-projects, confer as you go, giving the boss the essential data and a chance to make changes. Immediately discuss any problem you can't handle.

(2) For long-term projects, agree on objectives and time frames before you start. Move confidently, but submit progress reports even if the boss didn't request them.

Ilsa has an excellent memory. She can pour out details of a conversation held three months ago and keeps reminding her staff of statistics they forgot. She has her assistant Sherri in a tailspin, trying to keep on top of orders and directives. Ilsa assigned Sherri to analyze a report on how a new government regulation will affect the organization. Sherri was pondering the best way to approach it to be sure to include whatever information Ilsa would need. Instead of waiting until it was done to respond, I suggested that Sherri immediately outline the paper and check in.

What to say If Sherri's not reading Ilsa correctly, it's better to straighten this out before she wastes her time and unleashes the boss's wrath.

> ***Sherri:*** "Ilsa, with your approval, I'll prepare the paper you suggested by next Wednesday. Please indicate any changes you want on the proposed topic outline."

You can learn a great deal from a bright boss if you don't get intimidated by his arrogance and conceit. Show you are almost as quick, but still eager to learn.

Guiding the pompous, inept boss

From the arrogant but clever boss, turn 180 degrees and you'll find the pompous but inept boss. To veil a shaky self concept, these administrators love all the ceremonial trappings they can muster. Name plaques, framed certificates, and civic awards dominate their office decor. More than anything else, they want to look good and be recognized as very important people.

TIP: You can help yourself and your pompous, inept boss by ignoring the bluster and encouraging conversation and discussion. Everyone will benefit if you push the boss in the right direction.

Strategy Your objective is to nudge your boss toward doing the right thing.

As her assistant, Seth finds Pauline's behavior abrasive. If Seth wants to improve the situation, he has to put aside his annoyance and help Pauline tone down her boastful remarks and put good ideas into action.

What to say   Give your boss credit for approving an idea you've carefully placed for consideration. So what if it was your idea—the boss *did* approve it.

> **Seth:** "Pauline, the gang really liked your order for the new leave slips."
>
> "Pauline, here's some back-up information to look over before the Holstrom meeting. Once he observes your sense of fair play, you'll have his attention and respect."

The pompous, inept boss really needs your help and you'll learn a lot from the experience.

When the boss throws temper tantrums

With some bosses, you're always on red alert. While talking to the time bomb, you never know what's going to make him explode or even what lights the fuse.

> **TIP:**   Moody monarchs who are continually up in the air, then down in the doldrums, may need professional help. Certainly they destroy their own productivity and mislead everyone under them. If you think you're being threatened by these emotional outbursts, put some distance between you and your boss.

Strategy   Your immediate objective is to calm down the boss who's having a temper tantrum. Give him a few minutes to rant on and hopefully he will wind down as you listen quietly.

Dawn can be having a nice, quiet debate with her boss when, snap, Sam becomes argumentative and his mood escalates to anger and rage. It's pointless to continue. Above all, she can't tell him he's wrong because that would only increase his anger.

What to say   If the boss calms down, you can try to resume the discussion.

> ***Dawn:*** "Sam, from my experience, it seems to me that such an approach might have the opposite effect—"
>
> ***Sam:*** (interrupting) "No, impossible. Only an idiot would say that, and if you can't—"
>
> ***Dawn:*** (interrupting him in a soft voice) "Just a minute, boss. Please sit down and let me finish the point I was making."

On the other hand, if Sam becomes more abusive, Dawn should quickly end with:

> ***Dawn:*** "We'll finish this some other time."

If walking away isn't enough, consider walking to another office—permanently.

When your boss's indifference creates a leadership vacuum

Some bosses carry non-interference to the point of disinterest. When conditions reach this extreme, someone usually leaps forward to fill the leadership vacuum.

TIP: A boss who doesn't want to take the lead may be happy to have you tell him where he's going.

Strategy When you decide to fill the leadership vacuum, your objective is to keep everything out in the open. No hide and seek and no deception. Instead, you can offer your boss a carefully thought-out plan.

Lisa seized an opportunity to advance a giant step. Since most people prefer the safer game of follow-the-leader, the rest of the staff began to look to her for the guidance they needed. She did this with her boss's knowledge.

What to say Lisa offered a detailed proposal which the boss approved with minor modifications.

Lisa: "Boss, I've developed some ideas concerning our department for your review. Here's a planning calendar of proposed projects for the year. and here's a pert chart showing what steps we could take each month toward achieving our objectives."

Lisa gained invaluable experience she later used when she became the head of another department.

* * *

In dealing with difficult bosses, no matter how disappointed, hurt, or angry they make you, you're not going to change them by getting even. Seek an unemotional solution that can benefit you both. Make your time under their leadership as tolerable as possible. When it becomes intolerable, if you can't change the circumstances, change your office.

CHAPTER 2

$$\left(\right)$$

The Three Principles of Complaining to Achieve Your Aim

QUIZ #2. DO YOUR COMPLAINTS GET RESULTS?

Are you talking out of reason or just reacting emotionally when something goes wrong on the job? Look more closely at yourself. What would you most likely say in the following situations? An interpretation of your choices follows.

1. For the third time, items you ordered were never shipped because authorization was buried on the boss's desk. You

    (a) say nothing, keeping your frustrations bottled up.
    (b) try to suggest procedural changes to the boss.
    (c) keep quiet—you can't change the boss's bad habits.

2. The boss indicated each assignment he gave you is important. Some, however, are quite time-consuming. You

    (a) say nothing, guessing at what to tackle first.
    (b) say nothing, starting with the assignment that's on top.
    (c) ask the boss for the order of priority.

3. Nothing was said, but you sense you've displeased the boss. You

   (a) immediately discuss this with your boss.
   (b) ignore the feeling without comment, waiting to receive your annual formal evaluation.
   (c) carefully avoid speaking to the boss whenever possible.

4. At the last staff meeting you commented on a problem about which you had little factual data. But you know

   (a) you should have boned up beforehand on the agenda.
   (b) you can get by speaking in generalizations.
   (c) that logical talk alone can make you sound good.

5. You're not being compensated for all your responsibilities. You

   (a) issue an ultimatum—fair compensation or you'll quit.
   (b) shrug this off—it's par for the course.
   (c) document recent accomplishments for future talks.

6. The boss hands you another assignment that "must get done immediately" when you're already under deadline pressure. You

   (a) drop everything to work on the new assignment.
   (b) ask the boss to adjust your workload.
   (c) say nothing, staying late all week to get it all done.

7. You devised what you thought was a great proposal. The boss reacted pessimistically. You

   (a) ask the boss to explain his concerns to you.
   (b) decide to present the next proposal with a few cohorts to share the good or bad reaction.
   (c) decide you won't stick your neck out any more.

8. After you point out to your boss that something cannot possibly work, she insists on doing it anyway. You

   (a) request that the assignment be given to someone else.
   (b) cheerfully follow orders to the letter, documenting everything to protect yourself.

(c) reluctantly do what you are told quietly.

9. The boss confuses you, sometimes approving and sometimes disapproving the *same* procedure. You

    (a) ignore whatever he says and do what you think is right.

    (b) ask your boss for a clear explanation before proceeding.

    (c) guess at his meaning and act accordingly.

10. You anticipate potential problems with an idea the boss proposed enthusiastically for staff discussion. You

    (a) say nothing, fearing your criticism might threaten the boss's authority.

    (b) take a stand against the proposal anyway.

    (c) keep still to keep the boss from opposing any idea you come up with.

Interpretation

1. If you are too quick to give up or don't try to cope, you're obviously not getting desired results. Suggest possible ways to improve the situation.

2. By guessing or working without direction, your boss may accuse you of neglecting the most important task. Ask the boss in what order to tackle it all.

3. With the slightest hint that the boss is displeased, protect yourself and find out. Otherwise, you either continue doing something wrong or you are worrying needlessly.

4. You win more respect for your argument if you can back it up with the facts. Most people can see through bluffing.

5. Threaten to leave and you'll find you're not indispensable; however, doing nothing isn't being fair to yourself. Prepare to argue your case in a professional manner before requesting a wage adjustment.

6. Don't assume your boss knows your deadlines or that you feel overworked. It is up to you to report the workload problem and let the boss adjust it by postponing deadlines, transferring work, giving you a helper, and so on.

7.   You get points for trying even if you didn't hit it right, but learn from any mistakes you made. Teaming up with others is all right, but you still need to know the boss's objections.

8.   Your duty is to point out pitfalls to the boss. The boss's duty is to decide whether to proceed. Once the decision is made, as long as it's legal and moral, it is your job to carry it out as cheerfully as you can. However, if you fear getting blamed for failure, protect yourself by documenting each step.

9.   You can't proceed with mixed messages. Get clarification from your boss or you will eventually be blamed for something not your fault.

10.   Being a "yes-man" is of little value to your boss. If you criticize tactfully, the boss will appreciate hearing potential flaws he may have overlooked. It's a greater risk to be a sycophant than a trusted advisor.

HOW GRIPING CAN RESULT IN POSITIVE CHANGES

Most of the time there's something you can say to make a troublesome situation better. If you suffer in silence, your bottled-up anger will eventually make you explode at the wrong time. What's worse, by saying nothing, you encourage the same condition to persist. Wherever you work, you'll find certain systems, orders, and regulations that keep you from doing your job well, or as well as you could.

But you're not powerless. Learn to strengthen your legitimate complaint and, at the same time, soften your tough language. By offering to help, not harm, your words won't be perceived as menacing. To complain successfully without incurring the boss's wrath, understand that everybody has to win something. Remember these three principles:

- Think before you speak
- Disagree professionally
- Use tact to get what you want

Think Before You Speak

Don't shoot from the lip. Unless there's an unexpected crisis, you have time to gather information before making a decision. You might get away with spouting off once or twice before you're ready, but soon others will be wise to you. Calmly pounce on the problem. Acquire a penetrating knowledge and learn why precedents were established. Now you can talk.

Be prepared with the facts

Instead of stewing over a policy you disagree with, speak up and try to get it changed. Be prepared to quote from an authoritative report or study. Note how impressive you can be saying

> "According to the manager's most recent report, there's a 12 percent increase in turnover for this fiscal year. And in that 12 percent, over a fourth were highly trained technicians. ..."

Before your next staff meeting, study the agenda. (If agendas are not sent out in advance, suggest that they should be.) Bone up on any topic of great concern to your unit.

TIP: People pay attention to other people who are prepared. Most people don't take the time or the trouble to dig out data without being asked to do so. When you are knowledgeable due to your own initiative, you stand out like a blinking neon sign.

Strategy   Your objective is to convince the boss to do something else or do it another way. Your strategy is preparation. A basic rule for succeeding in making needed changes is to do your homework.

Carrie was building up a head of steam to have it out with her boss about a new directive with which she strongly disagreed. Carrie was advised to prepare her case. Carrie agreed to arm herself quickly with information, assembling persuasive facts.

What to say   Ready with an informed opinion based on available data and company goals, Carrie could now speak unemotionally.

Carrie: "Boss, if our aim is increased production, this directive might have the opposite effect. According to our records, last fall we. .."

It's foolish to fake it or to rely on an emotional outburst when you're much more effective with convincing data.

Ask your boss to determine priorities

Think you're overworked? Perhaps. Some bosses keep you going at a hectic pace because they give you too much to do. Most don't give you enough. And frequently the gremlin is uncoordinated assignments that waste a lot of time.

TIP: Your objective is to have a reasonable workload, having time to do first what the boss considers most important. When you are truly overworked, ask the boss to decide the order of priorities, adjust the load, or get you some help. Appeal to the boss's desire to have the job done properly.

Strategy   Develop your own bargaining tool.

(1) Make a list of what you are now doing, noting a rough weekly time estimate by each task.
(2) Check those items that fall outside of your job description.
(3) Ask the boss to look at the list and reapportion your time.

Newt was bristling because Karen, his boss, just delegated another task to him and there was no way he could get all that work done. Instead of Newt blurting out his annoyance to Karen, I suggested he prepare a Task/Time Estimate list. It's an easy way to find extra hours in a day and reduce the tension.

What to say   With the list clutched in his hand, Newt was now ready to deal.

Newt:	"Karen, am I right in assuming that this new assignment is pretty important to you?"
Karen:	"It sure is, Newt. I absolutely must have it by next week."
Newt:	"Well, boss, I've been trying to figure how I could make enough time available to do a really good job on it. This is what I'm doing now and the approx-

imate time it takes. With your permission, I can put the items I've checked on the back burner unless you want someone else to take care of them."

With one quick, pleasant, professional swing, Newt just placed the ball in the middle of his boss's court.

Keep your optimism in bounds

If your boss is always pessimistic, not giving you the inspiration and support you need after you've agreed on procedures or after a project falls flat on its potential, that's a legitimate basis for discussion.

> **TIP:** It takes more than one wet blanket to submerge a practical proposal imbedded in sound thinking. Even optimism can be overdone or out of place. Realism keeps your head above water.

Strategy Your objective is to get enough information about an idea before becoming optimistic. Ask for more details when the boss turns thumbs down on your proposal.

Otis is annoyed because whenever he comes up with a good idea, his boss, Miles, throws a wet blanket on it with comments such as:

Miles: "We can't do that. We don't have enough manpower."

"Now Otis, you know you don't have enough experience to try that."

Otis calls Miles a pessimist who doesn't know how to encourage his subordinates. Maybe. Or is Otis going off half-cocked?

What to say Otis needs more specific guidance from his boss if any of his suggestions are to see daylight.

> ***Otis:*** "Boss, please explain to me why you think my expectations are unrealistic."

Without this feedback, Otis could be repeatedly making the same error. Don't let your enthusiasm get ahead of your brain. Refrain from speaking until you think through a sticky situation.

Disagree Professionally

If your company were a democracy, you could push the self-correction button. You could just raise your hand to take a stand. Instead of everyone hailing the status quo, each idea would get pulled apart in competitive discussion. Some firms actually come close to operating like that. If yours doesn't, conserve the heat generated by all that pressure to conform. Cook up some alternatives. Gently suggest counter proposals. Look for offers the boss can't refuse.

How to stick your neck out without getting it chopped off

Some bosses believe the definition of agreeable is a person who always agrees with them. You find yourself walking a tightrope trying to oppose the boss without being branded a troublemaker.

TIP: Your objective is to deliver criticism without letting your boss feel that his authority or judgment is being questioned. Should that happen, your boss may get stubborn or display some other defensive behavior rather than being receptive to your suggestion.

Strategy   Approach your boss by carefully masking disapproval while emphasizing a positive, alternative move.

Valerie said she objected to the boss's idea because it would take too much time and consequently be too expensive. After thinking it through, she saw a faster way.

What to say   Valerie offered her suggestion as though the boss were part of finding the better solution.

Valerie: "Boss, your idea is good. You might be able to make it even better if you could come up with a way to reduce the time factor. Maybe we could try. . ."

To get the boss to look at additional factors in another situation, she nudged him with:

Valerie: "You know, boss, our thoughts are usually simpatico. You might want to kick around another possibility before you sign that. Perhaps you'd want to consider that it may have been poor job design and no feedback that caused the trouble."

Criticism veiled as a viable alternative is usually well accepted.

When your erring boss demands blind obedience

In some offices anybody who expresses an opposing idea is on his way out. It's corporate suicide not to blindly obey even when you're sure the procedure being advocated is wrong. There is so much stored up hostility, you feel like you're working with explosives about to blow. The message from the top echelon, as you interpret it, leaves you with two apparent choices—accept the procedure or move somewhere else.

TIP: In addition to acceptance or leaving, there is a third alternative—deliberately doing it "wrong" in order to bring about change. Give the bosses enough rope and they'll hang themselves on their own stiff and inflexible collars.

Strategy Your objective is to improve a bad regulation. This strategy comes from Abraham Lincoln who said that the best way to get rid of a bad law is to strictly enforce it. If you anticipate trouble and your supervisor has deaf ears, then reverse yourself. Carry out the order to the letter. If your original thinking is right, that's the fastest way to get changes made.

From his past experience, Elton is certain his latest assignment is mission impossible. It can't work. The company with whom they are about to sign a contract has a poor reputation and is notoriously late in filling orders.

What to say   The first step is to speak up, very carefully, before starting.

> **Elton:**   "Boss, remember when we had a similar situation with the Dobbin company? Do you think we might be asking for the same kind of trouble here?"
>
> **Gus:**   "No, Elton. Just follow the order."

Instead of banging his head on his desk or arguing, Elton accepts the boss's decision even though he knows it's going to be bungled.

> **Elton:**   "OK, Gus, if you're sure that's what you want to do."

But Elton has to be sure to cover himself as he goes forward. That requires keeping a record of all facts, dates, figures, or whatever documentation he may need. Such precautionary measures are essential to protect you from blame. Also, you have the data to make a good, objective evaluation after a reasonable time for a test. (There's always the possibility that the boss was right and the ordered action was great.) You are prepared for a non-judgmental, let the facts speak for themselves, review.

How to push the boss who procrastinates

You are feeling miserable because of a stalling boss who needs a push to accomplish what he's promised. Whether it's arranging for repair work or reading the proposal that's been buried on his desk for three weeks, you can't get him to move.

TIP: Express more concern for the boss and the company than for yourself. Without threatening, let the boss know that you are aware of other steps to take. In serious situations supervisors don't want their subordinates going the grievance route, and they'll realize this could occur if they don't get to work immediately.

Strategy   Your objective is to get your boss to act.

(1)   Point out why it is in the best interest of the boss to act or to change a situation.

(2)   Make it as painless as possible for the boss to resolve the matter.

When Carlotta left on maternity leave Robin began "temporarily" handling vital aspects of Carlotta's work as well as her own. Finding a replacement has been dragging on. Vicky, her boss, fibs about holding job interviews she actually cancels, and she gives other excuses for stalling the hiring process. Robin believes Vicky has no intention of paying another salary for as long as she can get away with it.

What to say   Robin is exhausted. She can't wait any longer to ask for help.

> ***Robin:***   "Vicky, there are some tax forms Carlotta took care of that are being neglected. We are going to find ourselves in a serious mess if we don't hire someone immediately to fill in until Carlotta gets back. I know this is what you've been wanting to do but you've been too busy. Tomorrow I am interviewing candidates. I'll find the best three, then you can choose the one you want."

For Robin to move Vicky to action, she had to talk about Vicky's problems, not hers, and about their mutual goal to do what's best for the company. In this case Vicky did not object to her subordinate's taking the initiative. Had she objected, Robin would have had to cancel the interviews unless her boss wanted to conduct them herself.

TIP: If your boss doesn't follow up on a promised action, talk it out and come to some agreement. Then prepare a memo of your understanding of this agreement, sending the original to the boss, a copy to anyone else involved, and keeping a copy for yourself. This back up now prevents reneging later. Also, if you misunderstood, you'll be corrected and won't have unreasonable expectations.

How to press the boss to explain mixed messages

Some bosses seem to talk out of both sides of their mouths. One minute they're supportive and appreciative and the next, they're annoyed or displeased with you. You try to read the handwriting on the wall, but can't interpret the ambiguous picture.

TIP: Get the facts first. Don't accuse your boss of being two-faced or jump to conclusions. You have to keep working there, at least for a while, and maybe you'll hear a good explanation.

Strategy Your objective is to learn where you stand so that you can take any necessary corrective action. Ask your boss to give you some feedback.

Tyler, the head of the office, has been assuring Eric that his work is top notch. But Eric just learned that Tyler sent a memo throughout the office which omitted Eric's name and a few others as members of the influential planning committee. This came without warning or explanation. Maybe it was carelessness (forgetting to explain it to Eric) or insensitivity (thinking Eric wouldn't mind). Or maybe Eric was not as valued as he thought he was.

What to say Whatever the reason, Eric has to press his boss for an explanation.

> *Eric:* "Tyler, I'm getting mixed messages that I'd appreciate your deciphering for me. On the one hand, you tell me I'm doing excellent work. Then I read in a memo that I've been removed from the planning committee. Of course you have every right to say who should be on the committee, but frankly, I'm confused about the way I learned your decision."

Eric had gained nothing by guessing and had to get the facts. As it turned out, Tyler apologized, explaining that Eric's name was inadvertently omitted from the list.

When you can't talk to your boss about your problem

Sometimes your problem *is* your boss. Some bosses were never trained to supervise and their method of motivating is to take away the carrot altogether ("Do as I say or else. . ."). Some reveal a prejudice which you may be able to prove but that's a tough fight that can take years before anything is settled in court. Before you even think about litigation, go after immediate relief.

TIP: If you *really* can't talk to your boss about the problem, reduce the risk by getting a group together. This works only if the boss doesn't feel you are ganging up to present a threat. You might also consider going to your boss's supervisor to ask for advice, bringing tangible proof of your allegations. However, this too might backfire because the top boss will usually back up your boss.

Strategy Your objective is to bring about positive changes. When you're in a situation where you fear reprisal, this is one time you have to resort to anonymity with unsigned memos to the boss, letters-to-the-editor in the company newsletter, cartoons on the bulletin board, and so on.

Although she knew females in other departments of the company who had moved up, MaryLou believed that both her boss and her boss's supervisor treated women contemptuously and effectively blocked their advancement.

What to say Because the problem was not a company policy, but an attitude within her department and division, MaryLou decided to communicate anonymously with the president of her company sending him a message that:

1. she liked and wanted to continue working for the company;
2. her division and department directors were abusive and became more tyrannical if anyone complained; and
3. she urged improved supervisory training along with a company policy stating how anyone who does not treat

employees fairly and respectfully would be handled through the establishment of arbitration committees.

It was a last resort, but it did start some changes. MaryLou now believes that company presidents actually do read their mail.

Use Tact to Get What You Want

The more agreement you have before you start an assignment, the less hassle you have getting your job done. If you and your boss are clear on precisely how your job fits into company goals and unit objectives, you'll have less to complain about later on.

Don't issue an ultimatum unless you're willing to wave goodbye

You are in a fury. You just heard somebody else was assigned the project promised to you. In a situation like this, you're ready to demand your rights—or else! Nobody wants to be threatened. From the point of view of the company, this kind of threat seriously questions your loyalty. After all, wouldn't a loyal employee do everything possible to help, not harm, the company?

> **TIP:** The worst part about issuing an ultimatum is that you usually find out you are not as indispensable as you think you are. Say you're leaving and don't be surprised if the boss waves goodbye.

Strategy   Your objective is to change the boss's mind without losing your temper or your job.

(1) Consider alternative plans that could meet the immediate needs of the unit as well as your own.

(2) Make an appointment or at least calm down before you talk to your boss.

Anita had been planning for almost a year to go to Alaska on her annual vacation when she received word that she'd have to postpone her trip in order to design an important new project. She was on the verge of storming into the boss's office, telling him off with "I'll quit if you don't. . ." But what will that accomplish? I asked her. You may lose a good job and the company may lose a good worker.

What to say Show appreciation for being chosen and suggest a substitute.

> ***Anita:*** "Boss, I'm honored that you want me to work on the century project and I know i'd enjoy the challenge. You probably don't know I've had reservations for the past six months for my vacation to Alaska, so I'd like to suggest that Dustin head the new project instead of me. You can be sure he will do an excellent job."

Remember that your boss's primary obligation is to the company, not to you. Therefore, don't "tell off" your boss, but rather tell him how your option will work just as well.

How to get recognition for the work you do

When you started your job, your boss handed you a job description and you assumed that was what was expected of you. Why didn't someone let you in on the joke? Job descriptions and actual work are seldom synonymous. But there's no need to threaten the boss to find a satisfactory solution.

TIP: Your objective is to re-align your assignments more closely with the type of work you want to do and what you thought you'd be doing. Prepare to negotiate—list your activities, analyze, then sensitize your boss.

Your strategy is a tradeoff, a win/win negotiation

(1) Offer to give up something the boss thinks you want to do (that is actually not high on your priority list) in exchange for something you really do want. Or,

(2) Agree to take on a task that is apparently very important to your boss (something that you don't mind doing) that the boss doesn't want to do.

A year ago Gladys hired Marcia as an assistant whose primary responsibility was to study the department's operation and recommend changes to increase output and enhance quality. In the interval, Gladys has delegated to Marcia several nonrelated tasks that others without her expertise could do as well. Marcia feels these activities are taking her away from her goal—she wants experience in this position to help her move up to the CEO's prestigious Productivity Unit. She also noted that her boss really liked her recommendation that Gladys distribute weekly motivational pieces, but was putting off writing them.

What to say   Marcia sensed her boss really wanted the motivational pieces but needed help with them. This was a chance to trade.

> ***Marcia:***   "Boss, because my job has evolved into something other than what's in the job description, I'd like to review how you think I'd be of most help to you. As much as I enjoy compiling statistics from the divisions, I wonder if you'd rather I concentrate on producing several kinds of motivational pieces that…"

Everyone should come away from negotiation winning something he wanted. When your job description and actual work are too far apart to suit you, negotiate with your boss to reshape your duties. Tell your boss how to get what he wants in exchange for what you want.

Learn the score without waiting for your evaluation

Your annual formal work performance evaluation should come as no surprise. If your boss hasn't been giving you frequent informal feedback, you can't wait for Judgment Day to learn how you're doing. Both big and little concerns can affect your grade. Maybe your boss sees red whenever you wear your orange shoes. Or you drive her nuts playing with your hair while you're talking. Or he thinks your work is sloppy. Or you spend too much time on matters that shouldn't matter.

TIP: Your objective is to learn as soon as possible anything that displeases your boss so that you can correct it immediately. Arrange a time when the boss can afford a few minutes to talk to you without interruption. Determine what day of the week and time of day the boss is generally in a good mood with time to talk.

Strategy

(1) Do a quick analysis when you suspect something's wrong.

- What part of my work does the boss seem to value most?
- Where am I weak or vulnerable?
- How did the boss react last time I went in?
- What pleases or annoys the boss?

(2) Outline and rehearse the points you want to make.

Ever since her boss, Adam, asked Nora to make presentations for the company, she was getting behind in her other work. She sensed the boss was annoyed with her and wasn't sure if that was the reason. After she decided to talk to Adam about her progress or lack of it, I suggested that Nora carefully prepare rehearsing at home with a tape recorder, listening as though she were the boss to spot places where she could be more convincing.

What to say   First, probe for information, then strive for necessary adjustments.

> **Nora:** "Boss, I have the feeling something is wrong. I really want to turn in good work. If there's something I can correct, please tell me what you want done or undone."
>
> **Adam:** "Well frankly, Nora, it seems to me that you're proceeding at a snail's pace."
>
> **Nora:** "I know, Adam. The new account presentations mean I'm out of the office at least six hours a week. Do you want me to continue. . .?"

Once you know how your boss evaluates your work, you can spar openly without the risk of being knocked out on a technicality.

* * *

I gripe. You gripe. They gripe. In this declension the verb may be the same but the verve varies. And so do the consequences, depending on how you voice your complaint. By charging in, demanding or threatening, you seldom get what you want and even if you do, resentment lingers. Control your emotions and let your logic take over. In a calm, persuasive manner, present a plan or an alternative that will get the changes made and satisfy both of you.

CHAPTER 3

Preparing for
Presentations That Will
Win Points with Your Boss

QUIZ #3. ARE YOUR PRESENTATIONS WELL RECEIVED?

Before you give a talk—either before a small staff meeting or a major conference—consider the myriad of points that can increase your effectiveness. Learning from your past experiences, use the following checklist to mark the items you feel need more of your attention.

When introducing a speaker:

( ) Do you keep it short, whetting not satiating the appetite?

( ) Do you personalize, telling some characteristic the audience can relate to?

( ) Are biographical items germaine to audience and topic?

( ) Are you gracious without overselling the speaker?

( ) Do you save the speaker's name until the very end of the introduction?

( ) Do you keep eye contact by memorizing or rehearsing, and not reading the introduction?

When planning a presentation:

( ) Is it based on notes made from time to time instead of knocked out at one sitting?

( ) Does your topic coincide both with your desired outcome and audience interest?

( ) Do you work from an outline—introduction, main idea, few supporting points and conclusion?

( ) Do you start by involving the audience, a warm up before swinging into the subject?

( ) Do you avoid starting with an apology or a joke?

( ) Are the content and vocabulary geared to audience intelligence, interest, and background?

( ) Have you pared your prepared remarks to fit the audience attention span, with remaining time for their questions?

( ) Is your talk planned for the ear, with conversational vocabulary, as though having an animated chat with friends?

( ) Do you plan an emphatic closing, ending with a punch?

When delivering the talk:

( ) Do you strive for a simple, uncluttered personal appearance not to detract from the talk?

( ) Do you wait for quiet, absolute attention, before beginning?

( ) Do you avoid detracting mannerisms—playing with tie, jewelry, jingling change in the pocket, and so on?

( ) Do you adjust the mike to chin level and avoid shouting?

( ) Do you maintain constant eye contact with audience?

( ) Have you memorized no more than the opening and closing paragraphs?

( ) Do you speak from key-word notes both to trigger memory and to keep spontaneity?

( ) Do you emphasize essentials by pausing, lowering the voice, spreading out words, or restating the point?

( ) Do you keep going, not stopping to correct mistakes unless it's essential to the meaning?

( )If there's no lectern, can you keep hand-held paper from rattling?

( )Can you handle the heckler who won't be ignored?

( )Do you know how and when to use visuals with your talk?

HOW TO SPEAK TO AND FOR THE TOP BRASS

Speaking in public is just glorified person-to person conversation. Only your listeners talk back to you with a smile or a scorn, a nod or a shake, or by clapping or napping. You also speak louder and maybe into a microphone and you've carefully thought out everything you are going to say.

Many top executives consider good communication skills a foremost quality if you want to move up in business. Fortunately, these skills can be learned. Whether enlightening the big brass on your special project, making a presentation at your sales meeting, or talking to a community group about the work of your organization, here is help with

- Introducing your boss or another speaker
- Essential factors in planning presentations
- Making a good impression when you deliver your talk

Introducing Your Boss or Another Speaker

You may have to introduce your boss at a large formal dinner, or your assistant to your management team, or a guest at your staff meeting. The same techniques apply for all of these situations. Polish your proficiency because how you introduce a speaker reflects upon you, your unit, and your company.

Three easy steps to introductions

The worst mistakes people make when introducing speakers are (1) they say too much, giving the talk for the speaker, and (2) they say the wrong things—extraneous, irrelevant, and impersonal information.

> **TIP:** An introduction should merely whet the appetite, not satiate it. A few choice nibblers are more appealing than an overwhelming array.

Strategy Your objective is to be impressive by conveying concisely what the audience wants to know. S.I.P. is an easy three-step formula for concocting a good introduction.

(1) Let "S" stand for the *subject* of the talk.

(2) Add "I," for the *interest* of the audience in that subject

(3) And "P" for the *person* who will be talking.

Denise invited a financial consultant to speak to her Directors' Meeting. She wanted help in preparing her introductory remarks.

What to say Following the formula, I cautioned her to give just a smattering about the topic, to point out its relevance to her directors, and to select a few pertinent items about the person she had picked to speak.

> **Denise:**   (S)"You've heard that there's a merit increase plan under consideration and a lot of rumors have been circulating..."
>
> (I)"We realize you're anxious to know how you and your people will be affected and when..."
>
> (P)"Our guest today is considered tops in the field of financial planning by his own peers who presented him their equivalent of an academy award...His string of accomplishments is long enough to reach around the room, yet he impresses you as someone who doesn't care a whit for recognition. But I know all of you will recognize his wit as you enjoy listening to our guest, John Banter."

Remember, give your listeners a sip instead of a mouthful.

How to be gracious without overselling

To do right by your speaker, follow these seven pointers.

1. *Be selective in what you say about the person* Even if the speaker is your boss, forget the five-page biography. An introduc-

tion is no time for a lengthy talk filled with irrelevant items. Unless the speaker is talking about sports, nobody cares that he played college basketball. The more well known your speaker, the less you say, as in

> "Ladies and gentlemen, the President of the United States."

2. *Close with a personal characteristic* Perhaps you can talk about the speaker's ability to put everyone at ease or her enthusiasm. For example:

> "She's such a dynamic and exciting person, I've been taking tons of B-12 and I still can't keep up with her."

3. *Be charming without alarming the speakers* Don't load them down with impossible-to-live-up-to praise, such as

> "Here's the most amusing speaker you've ever heard."

4. *Poke fun only at yourself* Avoid humor at the expense of any group or individual. Poking fun at the speaker is risky even if she's a close friend. What is a simple jest to you can be an offensive sting to your guest or to your audience. If you must poke, let the joke be on you.

5. *Be original* "The man who needs no introduction" deserves better than that overworked salute. To avoid being trite, consult books filled with epigrams, witty sayings, anecdotes, and quotations.

6. *Be brief* When you go over two minutes, you rob the speakers of some of their allotted time, make the speech for them, upstage them, become irrelevant, or tire the audience so that the speaker starts with two strikes. Since your talk is short, there's no excuse to read your introduction. Practice it until your remarks, although memorized, appear to be spontaneous.

7. *Get the name right and save it for last* Only at the very end do you mention the speaker's name. Otherwise, he or she is apt to pop up each time you say it thinking, "I'm on now." Be sure to check the pronunciation in advance. Then finish your introduction with the name, as in

> ". . .And now, please join me in welcoming Sherry Fervor."

Essential Factors in Planning Presentations

Don't try to knock out a talk in one sitting. Think about it as you do routine tasks. Clarify your thoughts and probe deeper by talking to those with opposing views. Debate silently with authors who've dealt with the topic.

Once you decide on a subject, it's almost mystical how it creeps into your conversation, magazine articles, and TV shows. Actually, your brain was alerted to be on the lookout. As you accumulate information, much more than you'll use, you begin to feel as though you are an expert on the subject. This self-confidence will be reflected in your talk. The audience senses it and they feel confidence in you.

How to blend your purpose with audience appeal

What do you hope your talk will accomplish? Do you want to suggest a solution, debunk some myths, sell your product, contract for services, or get approval for your proposal? Whatever it is, focus on the purpose. Then think about appealing to the particular audience you're going to address.

> **TIP:** Listeners want to know right away where you're headed. You can't fool them. They know the difference between a definite direction and a senseless rambling or meaningless smattering. Because they can't absorb too much at one time, find a common thread you can weave, *one main idea that a few major points can cling to.* You will illustrate and clarify these points in a variety of ways.

Strategy   While your purpose will change with each talk, your objective is to combine what you want to accomplish with audi-ence acceptance. The strategy is to keep your talk focused.

(1) Go through the motions of actually writing out your purpose.

(2) Determine what the group is interested in.

The boss arranged for Honey, her assistant, to speak before the Board on the project Honey had proposed. Because she had a lot riding on this talk, Honey wanted some advice. She agreed to write out her purpose.

> "My talk to the board should result in their tangible support for my project."

Next, to help her think about the members of the Board, I gave her five questions. From her responses, she figured out the group's prime interest.

1. What do they expect to get out of my talk?
2. How do they happen to be interested in this subject?
3. What's their understanding and sophistication level?
4. How much background information do I have to give them before I can launch into my main message?
5. What analogies or examples could they relate to?

In trying to relate to each particular audience, it's important to gauge and respect their intelligence. Otherwise your talk will be a disaster. If you go above their heads, you lose them. If your talk is too elementary, you insult them. Gear your vocabulary and explain your position on the level they can comprehend.

Building around the four main parts

The four parts of your talk are the introduction, main point, supporting points, and conclusion. Start your preparation with a rough outline.

(1) The Introduction. From your first words, you want your audience to feel that they are going to enjoy listening to you. Even if you're only talking at your own staff meeting, you want their instant involvement. Your introduction is the warm-up before you start swinging. It might be an experience or a quotation. Or try a question such as:

> "How many of you remember when. . .?"

Or a personal story:

> "I'm not superstitious, but I received an omen as I was driving here today. . ."

Or a reference to the audience or occasion:

> "Did you see the story on last night's TV news about. . .?"

Or you may prefer a dramatic statement, such as:

> "On Tuesday, when you vote for Proposal X, it's a waste of time." (pause) "That's what the opposition wants you to think. . ."

If you are to grab your audience with the first words of your introduction, here are three important reminders:

A. *Start in a positive way.* Don't apologize. We all have short-comings—don't advertise yours with

> "I'm not used to speaking."
> "I didn't have time to prepare."
> "I know I'm not as good a speaker as Bob Silver-tongue, but. . ."

B. *Use some opener other than a joke.* Unless you're an accomplished story teller, your joke may fall flat. Then you've lost the group's interest before you begin.

C. *Use new, refreshing material.* Don't repeat the trite expressions everyone has used, such as:

> "It's truly a pleasure to be invited to speak to such a distinguished group."

(2) The Main Point. Refer to your original notes in which you spelled out the purpose of your talk. That is your main point upon which you will elaborate. It is your message that you'll tailor to fit audience interest.

(3) Supporting Points. When sorting your notes, if you are ruthless in tossing out miscellaneous points that don't fit, you'll find you have three or four *major* categories. If you need more documentation, go to the library for additional facts, sayings, stories, or analogies.

An original quotation, more than a famous one, is sometimes better if it is more to the point. For example,

> "One of my clients remarked to me the other day that. . ."

Generously sprinkle specific cases and examples throughout your talk, especially illustrations that *this* audience may have experienced. Go light on numbers. Use statistics sparingly—only for impact or drama. But go ahead and make the important point you believe should be evident to everyone. It may not be that obvious. If it is, the audience enjoys hearing their ideas expressed your way. They will be thinking:

> "That's just what I've been saying." or "That's the way. You tell 'em, Harry!"

(4) Conclusion. End emphatically with any of the same types of appropriate attention-grabbers you considered in the introduction—an anecdote, dramatic statement, quotation, question, and so on. You can alert your audience that you're moving into your close with:

> "I'd like to leave you with this thought."
> "And finally I want to tell you what a fortune teller predicted about..."

The conclusion is your main idea summarized into a single punch. The point you want them to remember most or the action you want them to take. It should be obvious by your final line that you are finished with your talk.

Even though you probably won't use it in this form, draft your complete speech from your outline to get an idea about the length and how it holds together. This is also helpful for those instances when the talk is to be distributed and reprinted, when you want to submit excerpts to a professional journal or company newsletter, or your boss decides to enclose reprints with customer mailings.

Enhancing your individual style

When planning your presentation, the talk has to be tailored to fit you. These pointers should help you do this.

1. *Be yourself* You want to sound like you, not an imitation of anyone else.

2. *Talk for the ear, not the eye* Write out your talk conversationally in spoken rather than written vocabulary. Don't be afraid of contractions. That's how we speak. We also talk in the active, not passive voice.

3. *Be pleasant* Don't be clever for the sake of cleverness. It is better to give something to muse over for hours than to amuse for a moment.

4. *Save room for the spontaneous* Eliminate the extraneous. Red pencil lofty generalizations, hackneyed expressions, and meaningless phrases which will bog down your talk. Insert exciting verbs, adjectives, and adverbs that create images.

5. *Vary your sentences* Use many short and snappy ones without sounding staccato. Ask a question, then answer it. Talk about real people doing things.

Substituting a conversation for a speech

This is a technique that will allow you to enjoy the speaking experience without worrying about what comes next or if you left something out.

TIP: Use the conversation-instead-of-a-speech technique when you know your subject so well that you can field whatever questions are thrown at you. You'll be more animated and spontaneous. Your objective is to give the most pertinent information in a friendly, informal, enjoyable manner.

Strategy Prepare only your opening and closing. After the opening, immediately ask a question to involve the audience. Let the audience tell you what interests them through their questions.

Grant represented the office at a three-day conference. He dutifully wrote a good report but the boss now wants him to give the highlights to the whole group.

What to say Everything in the report is still fresh in his mind. He knows so much, he's going to have a difficult time narrowing down the information he gives. What he needs is a way to lead into a conversation.

> "We covered so much ground at the conference that I compiled my notes into this report that you can look at later. Right now, let's concentrate on what is of greatest interest to you—the state of the art

equipment, production methods, and innovations. What, especially, would you like to hear about?"

You'll find the conversation technique to be more enjoyable for you as well as for the audience.

How to be selective in using visuals

Good visuals support and clarify your point and enhance your talk. Inappropriate visuals destroy animated contact between you and the audience. Decide if your presentation could be more effective with attractive aids such as:

- charts and graphs—simple and uncluttered. These are effective when showing conditions and stages of progress.
- before and after photos—blow up some to poster size
- enlarged cartoons, reprints, and headlines
- table-top models
- overhead transparencies
- flipcharts and blackboards
- slides, films, and video tapes
- handouts distributed *after* your talk—a plastic or colored cover is impressive.

Delivering Your Speech with Poise

Sitting on the sofa among friends, your words tend to flow. On the job, you stick to the issues and, if it's a large group, you stand up to speak. It is the standing up and being the target of so many pairs of eyes that's unnerving. Consider this: If anyone else were better qualified to make your presentation, he or she would be doing it instead of you. You know more about what you are going to say than anybody else. For the moment, you are the authority and you have their attention.

How to control your nervousness

Even public speakers who talk every day may feel butterflies before they begin. It's a positive sign of excitement, an inner tension that gives a speaker sparkle. The audience senses your intense desire to reach them.

> **TIP:** While it's normal to be nervous, don't broadcast your mistakes. Your nervousness is much more noticeable to you than to anyone else. If you fluff, don't correct it unless doing so is essential to the meaning. When you hear yourself "uh" and "um," close your lips until you decide what you're going to say next. If you have to read a quote from a paper that begins to rattle because you're shaking, grab the paper firmly with both hands, each hand tugging gently in opposite directions.

Strategy   Your objective is to control your nervousness.

(1) Practice from a key-points outline, avoiding word-for-word memorizing to sound more spontaneous. Too many ad libs, though, will throw off your timing and you may forget the point you wanted to make.

(2) Memorize only the opening—a crucial time for capturing or losing the audience—and the closing so as not to kill a good talk with a flat finish.

(3) Feel more control, as well as achieve emphasis where needed, by going slower, louder, or pausing for effect.

J.L. wanted to know how to prevent his knees from banging together, a nervous stomach, nightmares, and a nasty blotch of hives whenever he had to give a talk. I suggested that he give himself enough time to prepare and practice his talk before a good friend. To prepare for answering questions after the talk, J.L.'s friend should ask him the most difficult questions they both can imagine.

Being well-groomed also preserves the nerves. Don't be the plumed peacock. Aim for the neat, uncluttered look with well-fitting clothes, buttoned jacket, no frayed cuffs, scuffed shoes or stocking runs. You want the concentration on your words, not your wardrobe.

Although some inner tension adds to your effectiveness, the negative nervousness you don't want to show is the fear of making a fool of yourself. The terror of thinking, "When I open my mouth, will I sound ridiculous?" You won't if you've organized your thoughts and planned what you'll say.

Incorporating your natural body language

How you gesture and move your body while waiting to speak and while you're talking influences the reaction to your presentation.

Your objective is to move smoothly. The answer is to practice at home and here are several tips:

1. *Break up your practice sessions* Don't overtire yourself practicing all at once.

2. *Check your facial expressions and posture in a mirror* Change your expressions to go with your words. A smile compliments your audience, so practice smiling each time you rehearse. You'll look good even if you feel tense.

3. *Rehearse standing up straight* Stand comfortably erect with your feet a little apart to avoid swaying or shuffling from one foot to the other.

4. *Be aware of distractions* Be careful not to fidget with papers, play with a button or jewelry, repeatedly jerk your eyeglasses on and off, run your fingers through your hair, push back a lock of hair, jingle change in your pocket, lick your lips, or pace back and forth.

5. *Hold on to something* Sometimes you will be giving your presentation in a small conference room where there is no lectern. If everyone is sitting around the table, rise to give your talk. Stand behind your chair and, if you feel nervous, firmly grip it with both hands to regain composure. If you give your report from the front of the room, you can grip the table.

TIP: While waiting to be introduced, sit straight with your hands in a natural position. Before you speak, smile and take a few deep breaths to appear poised as you collect your thoughts.

Look at the audience, and keep on looking at the audience, not at the floor or out the window. Find a few friendly faces and speak to them until you feel comfortable about moving your head from side to side to talk to everyone in the room.

Adjusting the seating, lectern, microphone, and timing

The Seating If you're talking to a very small group, you might sit among them as part of a circle. If you stand before a few rows, get right down there next to them. Should people be scattered throughout a half-filled room, say:

> "Come on down, there are seats here in front. You'll be able to hear better. Please join us."

Then stand there, smiling, waiting. Eventually someone will start the move to close ranks. When you aren't sure if the audience is receiving you, it's perfectly all right to ask,

> "Can you hear me in the back?"

The Lectern Place a copy of your notes on the lectern. You can glance down but for a second at a time and yet keep your place, allowing almost as much eye contact as you'd have in ordinary conversation. The lectern isn't a life preserver—don't clench it with a death grip.

The Microphone Don't play with the mike. Arrive a little early and note how to adjust it. Lower it below your chin height so that you speak over the top and not directly into it. It is ear-splitting to shout. If you find yourself behind a lectern that's too tall for you and you can't adjust it, stand to one side. The audience wants to see your face as well as hear your words.

The Timing Audience attention evaporates quickly. Unless you're a dynamic spellbinder, twenty minutes is the extent that they can sit still without wriggling. In accepting an assignment to speak, ask:

> "What time am I scheduled to speak?" "How long would you like me to talk?" "Would you like a question and answer period?"

You can adjust the length of the Q & A session so that your talk itself isn't too long. As you plan your talk, you'll be thinking about how much you can reasonably cover in the allotted time.

How to respond to hecklers

Hecklers are determined to call attention to themselves by shouting unpleasant comments or questions.

TIP: Hecklers want to get you into an argument and cause you to get angry and blow your cool. When you get zinged with a hostile question, turn away, look at someone else, and rephrase the query.

Strategy Your objective is to retain control. The strategy is to restate the heckler's point or concern. This gives you time to think up an answer.

Patty asked me how to handle unfriendly heckling. We worked on a barb tossed at her that morning.

> ***Heckler:*** "You have a lot of nerve coming here today when last year you promised us that..."

What to say You can't always ignore hecklers. Give them a little spotlight, then turn away.

> ***Patty:*** "The question is: Am I taking a different position today than last year? Yes, I am, in this way and for this reason:..."

You don't have to be funny or clever, just get rid of the question and call on the next person. If you have no answer, be honest:

> "I really don't know the answer to that. I'm going to have to research it and get back to you later."

In the audience you're apt to find *Smilers* (speaker's pets whose smiles give you instant encouragement) and *Nodders* (they agree and let you know it. Ah, right on target). Concentrate on them and discipline yourself not to be distracted by these other types:

Headshakers They disagree and let you know it. Thanks for listening, you'll answer them later.

Cold-Starers They pierce you with "I dare you to make it good."

PurseSnappers An open and shut case.

Asiders They're afraid their neighbors can't catch on without their comments, or that maybe your tie would miss their eye.

Squirmers They look like they sat on a pile of red ants.

Nervous Coughers They fight fright for you. Thanks, but no thanks.

Early Leavers They forget the knack. The back's for quick getaways.

* * *

A few people have the talent to get away with highflown speeches delivered on formal occasions. Most people don't. So skip the oratory at formal award banquets and especially at the office. Just concentrate on conversing with your audience. Simply talk as one person to another, whether you're addressing 3 or 300. You can improve your presentations by rehearsing at home, tape recording yourself, and adjusting your speed, tone, volume, rhythm, and enunciation. With enough practice, you'll be an effective speaker.

CHAPTER 4

Four Strategies That Favorably Shape the Boss's Perception of You

Fill in your own report card. No one else will see this, so be perfectly honest in grading yourself on how well you're coming across to impress the boss. "A" means you're doing great; "B" is okay, but could be better; "C" says you want to improve in that particular area.

	A	B	C
1. You communicate major skills top executives look for—seeing the broad picture, making quick decisions, and getting results.	( )	( )	( )
2. You think of yourself as a product to be sold, a total package to be merchandised.	( )	( )	( )
3. You appear secure and don't resort to extremes to call attention to yourself.	( )	( )	( )
4. You practice speaking by listening to yourself on recorded tapes.	( )	( )	( )

5. You can be forceful without being dog-
   matic.   ( ) ( ) ( )
6. You avoid quick, jerky moves, sitting
   on the edge of your chair, and other
   body language that shouts you are feel-
   ing nervous.   ( ) ( ) ( )
7. You speak politely to everyone, having
   the same manner for the messenger as
   for the manager.   ( ) ( ) ( )
8. You use office gatherings to make im-
   portant contacts and you talk there
   knowing higher-ups are observing you.   ( ) ( ) ( )
9. Your conversation is animated, show-
   ing a high degree of energy and physical fitness from following good health
   habits.   ( ) ( ) ( )
10. You maintain visibility by speaking up
    at staff meetings on agenda items
    you've carefully studied.   ( ) ( ) ( )
11. You gain notice by submitting to the
    company newsletter, joining the
    speakers bureau, or working on the
    boss's pet project.   ( ) ( ) ( )
12. You remember to phone or write notes
    of appreciation and congratulations.   ( ) ( ) ( )
13. Your frequent smile says you are ob-
    viously getting satisfaction and pride
    from your work.   ( ) ( ) ( )
14. You propose concrete plans to back up
    your enthusiasm.   ( ) ( ) ( )
15. You always appear to be in control of
    yourself, avoiding talk about your per-
    sonal problems around the office.   ( ) ( ) ( )
16. You accept the blame without making
    excuses when one of your subordinates
    goofs up.   ( ) ( ) ( )
17. After being blamed for your boss's mis-
    take, you wait until the boss is calm
    and rational to objectively discuss al-
    ternatives.   ( ) ( ) ( )

18. You express excitement and eagerness to accept a new assignment or challenge. ( ) ( ) ( )

19. You hear the boss's constructive criticism as a compliment, knowing he wants you to improve and stay with the company. ( ) ( ) ( )

20. You indicate how your proposals relate to company priorities. ( ) ( ) ( )

21. You ask guidance from the one person in the office the boss most respects. ( ) ( ) ( )

HOW TO SAY WHAT THE BOSS WANTS TO HEAR

Don't hold your breath waiting to be discovered. When looking at all the employees, all your boss sees is a sea of faces. You have to wave your potential and anchor his attention on you.

Here are four strategies to help your boss see you in a more favorable light.

- Create the illusion of success
- Maintain visibility to the boss
- Present a positive attitude
- Sell your ideas

Create the Illusion of Success

Part of impressing bosses is smoke and mirrors. What you are is not nearly as important as what they think you are. They draw conclusions from the way you speak, move, and look. If you present the image of confidence and competence and convey a sense of mission—knowing you're meant to do something and committed to getting it done—you show you're willing to pay your dues. You needn't be the smartest one in the office as long as you're viewed as one who grasps the whole picture, makes quick decisions, and gets results.

Improving everyday speech as part of your total package

Some people who work diligently don't advance. They never think of themselves as a product, an entire package to be merchandised, yet their bosses notice things other than their job performance. Everyday speech plays an important part in that perception.

> **TIP:** How you speak is more important than what you say. Pick out a few role models among people the boss admires. Study their speech, notice when they're quiet, figure out why they impress you.

Strategy Your objective is to express yourself more effectively. Tape record talks with friends to hear for yourself how you're coming across to others, concentrating on areas needing improvement.

Fern is anxious to move up. Her work is excellent, she's well dressed, exuberant, expresses her thoughts well, enunciates clearly, but her everyday talking is holding her back. She has to leave her four-letter words at home even though her colleagues laugh at her dirty jokes at meetings.

What to say Fern has to slow down, quiet down, and stop monopolizing every discussion. She also has to practice being forceful without being dogmatic by substituting softer language:

> ***Fern:*** "You make a good point, but statistics show..."
>
> "It seems to me the only logical conclusion is..."

After listening to her taped conversations, Fern recorded imaginary conversations, redoing them until she was satisfied with the tone and pace. Within a few months after her transformation, Fern was suddenly "discovered" as a rising star. Marketing yourself means perpetually polishing your skills and seeking better ways to express your thoughts.

Letting body language tell what you're not saying

Your boss will catch clues if you aren't saying what your actions suggest. Your expression, eyes, tone of voice, shrugs, and other gestures are dead giveaways.

> **TIP:** To appear more confident, imitate the way successful people glide smoothly and move decisively. They sit and stand erect and self-assured in contrast with those who slouch and sway.

Strategy   Your objective is to let your body language say you can succeed at whatever you try. Hold your head up, straighten your backbone, and practice acting as though you already are successful.

Jerry makes quick, jerky moves and sits too close to the edge of his chair. He might as well have a sign across his chest reading "I am very nervous."

How to say it   Jerry practiced at home before his mirror until he learned how to sit comfortably and still lean forward a little to show that he's listening carefully and to make a point. He concentrated on looking at his reflection without glancing away and controlling the hand gestures he hadn't been aware of before.

Sounding animated draws your boss to you

An animated, excited quality works like a magnet to draw your boss to you. Your smile is a magnet because it says you like being there. Your boss believes your exuberance when you declare without a trace of doubt in your voice, "I know I can do it. What a great idea! Let's get going."

> **TIP:** Sounding animated requires a high level of energy. Increase your supply with good nutrition, exercise, relaxation, and by flowing with the tide. Don't squander your energy. Either resolve annoyances or stop steaming about things you can't control.

Strategy   Your objective is to be perceived as enthusiastic about your work. You can get yourself excited and experience more energy by celebrating little "successes."

(1) Develop your own system for rewarding yourself after you complete each major segment of your assignment.
(2) Conserve your energy and enthusiasm by changing negative reactions into positive words.

Irene was clever but overly cautious, annoying everyone with her wimpy comments ("Although we agreed, I believe we should think about this some more before we implement it.") As a result, she became the target of barbs from colleagues—delivered in front of the boss.

What to say Irene agreed to reward herself at the end of each segment of her work by devouring a luscious, forbidden brownie with her coffee. I also suggested that she imagine herself protected by a plastic shield from which piercing remarks would bounce off instead of penetrating. She learned not to accept negative comments, but to rebuff them with a smile and a simple

"You may be right."

With much self discipline, Irene managed to restore her confidence and vitality. She displayed her new animation at office gatherings, introducing herself, expanding her contacts, talking enthusiastically about her work. An executive was so impressed with her team spirit that she was offered a promotion.

Maintain Visibility to the Boss

Except in a very small office, your boss won't necessarily know everything you are doing. To impress the boss who doesn't know, get your name or your face in view as much as you can. Be where the boss is reminded of you or your work, however this approach will backfire if you are blatant or become a pest. Use finesse.

Getting noticed by speaking at meetings

Rather than complaining about boring meetings and wishing your boss were a better planner, help the boss while setting the stage for winning attention by asking politely:

> "Boss, do you think we could have an agenda for our staff meetings, distributed the day before, so that we'd be better prepared to discuss the issues?"

Now you can do your homework and take a more active role in the discussion. Most people will *not* do much advance studying. If you do, you stand out. By reviewing issues and formulating questions that put problems in better focus, you signal invaluable leadership that your boss will surely hear.

Getting noticed by volunteering

Ideally, volunteering combines satisfying your desire to serve with receiving some benefit in your work. For instance, chairing a charity fund-raiser and getting the committee to identify you with your firm when they publicize the event. A boss is usually impressed to learn that you're promoting the company's image.

TIP: Realistically, you have limited time for extracurricular activities in the office. Select carefully, looking first at whatever project the *boss* thinks is important.

Strategy Your objective is get the boss's favorable attention while you're doing some good for someone else.

(1) Volunteer for the boss's pet project. Create an opportunity for higher-ups to notice your organizational and motivational skills.

(2) Volunteer for projects that let you learn a skill or meet new people, such as coordinating the office picnic, blood drive, or United Way sign-up.

Merle completed her agency's speakers bureau training which helped her personal development and put her in a position to make friends for her agency all over the community. Her question was: How could she make sure the boss heard about her volunteer activities?

What to say I told Merle to fold this information into casual remarks gently.

> **Merle:** "Boss, when I was speaking yesterday to the chamber of commerce, they appeared very excited about our new project. They asked me to find out from you if..."

The boss was intrigued with Merle's initiative. Volunteering also may provide you with an opportunity to send thank you notes to co-workers who help you. They receive these so infrequently, you'll automatically be spoken about kindly—little tidbits that get back to the boss.

Getting noticed by talking through company channels

Assess company channels open to your self-expression. For example, watch for a photo opportunity about your unit's work for the company newsletter or annual journal and suggest a succinct quote or call to suggest a potential news story.

TIP: So few employees bother to take advantage of existing channels, you'll probably find your offer, contribution, or statement very well received.

Strategy Your objective is to become more aware of existing channels that can help you win approving nods from your boss.

(1) Send carefully calculated comments to the letters-to-the-editor column of the company bulletin, newsletter, or magazine.
(2) Offer to coordinate the program at an official company conference or after-hours function.
(3) Join influential committees and offer to draft reports.

Kerry submitted a one-page article to the company monthly, offering suggested changes to cope with a personnel problem. He hit on certain aspects of the retirement plan that were bothering many other employees. This resulted in a task force being formulated which led to a change in the regulations. Even though his article was unsolicited, it was controversial with company-wide interest, a combination newsletter editors look for.

More important to Kerry was the boss's reaction. Vi, his director, came up to him soon after publication and said:

Vi: "I've got to keep my eye on you, Kerry. You have some really good ideas."

Getting noticed by promoting yourself

You can also create new opportunities. If you had an experience that could help others, contribute your findings to professional or trade journals. Your boss reads them. If you're an expert on some subject, speak before community groups. Accept an office in a community organization. Your boss will hear about you.

TIP: Your objective is to blow your own horn with subtle, inoffensive, muffled toots. Hide your boasting beneath compliments you pay others. ("You know Hope is terrific. She could have taken all the credit for that cost-saving idea, but she shared it with me.") When attending out of office lunches, meetings, seminars, and conferences circulate, "work the room," and expand your external support network.

Strategy

(1) Broaden your contacts and exchange information. You may meet people who'll put in a good word to your boss or make you an offer.
(2) Publicize your professional accomplishments.
(3) Be a good loser—utilize a rejection as an opportunity.

Carla was feeling down because Warren, her boss, refused the proposal she submitted. I told her being a good loser this time may help her get what she wants next time.

What to say   I suggested an upbeat comment.

Carla: "Warren, I very much appreciate your considering the downtown proposal. I understand why it isn't timely, and you've helped me focus on our current priorities. Thanks again."

Warren: "I'm so pleased to hear you say that, Carla. It was evidently a good learning experience for you. Don't be discouraged. Feel free to show me your next idea."

Opportunities for self promotion are everywhere if you're alert to them. A frequently used technique is to convert the spoken compliment into a tangible asset. After someone lavishes praises to you about your fine work wishing there were some way to show appreciation, you say in a very modest tone:

> "Well, there is something you could do that could help me. Would you consider dropping a note or calling my boss? As department head, he would surely appreciate knowing you thought your case was handled well. And I certainly would be grateful to you."

Telling you is nice for your ego, telling your boss is good for your career.

Present a Positive Attitude

Having a positive attitude is as important to you in the office as a hammer and nails are to a carpenter. You always have the choice of being happy about your work or being miserable. Often you determine how your day will go. You are able to control many actions that are self-defeating such as staying off the phone for personal calls. You also can control smiling easily and often, and being pleasant to be with.

Stay professional—don't discuss personal problems

No one's interested in every detail of your private life. If baring your soul and your sorrows is all you contribute to conversations, you'll find yourself alone because you make other people feel uncomfortable. It is especially bad to tell your boss more than your boss wants to know.

TIP: Talking openly about personal matters may jeopardize your advancement. It takes too much time away from work, and your boss may figure if you speak so openly about private matters, you probably can't be trusted to keep your mouth closed about company developments.

Strategy Your objective is to have your boss consider you dependable. Talk as if you are always in control. Don't discuss your personal problems unless you have to be excused for an emergency.

Although Sybil's boss is fond of her, Cecile has grown impatient constantly hearing about Sybil's drawn out divorce battle, chronic allergies, and her son's troubles.

> **Sybil:** "Carl is being totally unreasonable and spiteful. I don't know if we'll ever be able to work out a settlement and..."
>
> **Cecile:** "I know you're upset, Sybil, but we really have to get these reports out."

What to say Sybil has a definite need to talk out her personal problems, but personal matters should be exchanged between close personal friends or family members. Such discussions are out of place in the work place.

What to say when you are having a really bad day

It's difficult, but it's smart to be congenial even when you'd like to give in to a rotten mood. We all have our troubles.

TIP: Every type of work has its moments of tedium. If you'll get these out of the way first, when you're having a bad day, you can be looking forward to more exciting parts as you proceed.

Strategy When you have troubles, your objective is to separate yourself from the rest of the world until you're ready to make unemotional, rational decisions. Find a quiet spot to get away for a while.

Willie was having a really bad day. There was no door to close so that he could be undisturbed, and he desperately needed a little time and space to bounce back. He didn't want to take out his anger on his colleagues or tell his boss where to put the job.

What to say   Willie asked Dale to take his telephone calls, turned his chair around blocking entry to his desk, and hung a sign on it:

"I need 15 minutes alone and then I can talk to you."

Willie used this time to figure out why he was so upset and what options were open to him.

Taking credit and taking blame

Good or bad, whatever happens in your unit is your responsibility and you are accountable to your boss. You get the credit; you take the blame. You can prevent some mistakes by paying closer attention to alarm bells that go off in your head when, for instance, you start to turn in an assignment and feel something is not quite right. Double-check for accuracy.

> **TIP:**   When you make a mistake, or some one under you does, admit this to your boss. Own up immediately before it's perceived as a cover up and even minor blunders are blown out of proportion with dire consequences.

Strategy   Your objective is to correct errors and acknowledge good work within your sphere.

(1) When admitting responsibility, recommend ways to keep the error from recurring.

(2) Modestly share in the credit for causing something to get done. When reporting accomplishments, mention subordinates who carried them out.

Dean had given Maury instructions that were perfectly clear, but Maury blundered. There was no time to correct the mistake before Dean's boss had to be told. He had to hear it from Dean.

What to say   Dean came right to the point and stuck to the point of this meeting:

Dean: "Boss, I wanted you to be aware of a problem in my unit. Evidently, I didn't make my instructions

> clear enough and one of my workers didn't. . .It's too
> late to correct this blunder, but I think we can
> prevent such a thing from happening again if we
> were to change the system so that. . . Does that
> meet with your approval?"

We all love to listen to confessions because we all make mistakes. Most people are quick to forgive if you are genuinely anxious to atone. But you must mean it when you say you're sorry, and you must say it right away.

What to say when it's not your fault

Sometimes it's not anyone's fault. The building was evacuated because of a bomb scare and you didn't finish your work on time. What good is it to dwell on a calamity? When you're a success, you flip. When you flop, mop up the tears and go forward.

Face disappointments realistically. Use boners as building blocks. Decide what you can learn from the experience and let your sense of humor help you bounce back. Stop to muse when you get a bruise. Then brush off and rush off to do it better. Include your evaluation and recommendations with your report. Those involved will listen to the lesson.

What to say when it's your boss's fault

You're invaluable if you can catch ahead of time any mistakes the boss may make. If told to do something that doesn't make sense, restate it in your own words to be sure you understood correctly, politely pointing out your concern.

However, sometimes, the boss needs a scapegoat and you're it. Whatever you say you're in a no-win position, even if you convince him that he caused the error. Keep still. Later, when he's calm and rational, you can discuss the alternatives objectively.

What to say when you can't keep your promise

When you find you can't keep your promise, make other arrangements and inform the person you are disappointing, especially if that person is your boss. If you can't produce on time, do the responsible act without waiting for a lecture on incompetence.

> "Boss, I found it necessary to make alternative arrangements in order to get the work done that you need by this afternoon. When I saw I was tied up in an unanticipated delay, I called Shirley and asked her to prepare the report you requested. I hope that's OK with you."

Speaking graciously even under pressure

Another way to present a positive attitude is to show you're anxious to get started on an assignment. Express pleasure in being asked to do something you know will help the company.

TIP: If you think you might snap at your boss when under pressure to produce, remember your job was created to give back-up, make work easier, and make the boss look good.

Strategy Your objective is to keep calm when asked to do the impossible. Suggest an alternative or ask your boss to prioritize.

Kirk had planned to do something other than prepare a report that his boss now wanted done right away. Kirk's annoyance was evident.

> **Kirk:** "Boss, you told me to be at Honker's office this morning to go over the summary. I can't be in two places at the same time."

What to say Regardless of his protests, Kirk will eventually do what the boss wants. How much better if the boss sees him as a willing assistant.

> **Kirk:** "Boss, I'll be glad to. Is it all right if I delay the summary with Honker until I finish the report?"

Look at each directive as something the boss needs. Don't argue, help figure out how to get it done.

Accepting the boss's criticism with appreciation

When your boss criticizes, listen gratefully without getting defensive. The boss probably wants you to get ahead and is trying to help you.

TIP: Instead of making excuses, try it the boss's way. Your objective is to learn from your mistakes.

Strategy   Release the negative emotions you feel when you make a mistake. Vent your feelings to a good friend, get rid of the anger and disappointment you're holding onto, then examine the situation with your boss.

For two weeks Lee worked to get an account that fell through. He's been walking around with his chin on the ground, snapping at everyone. Colleagues who empathized with him at first are annoyed that he hasn't tried to pull out of his gloom. His boss put the matter in focus.

> ***Charlotte:***   "If you had taken a different approach, Lee, it might have worked. For example, if you had. . ."
>
> ***Lee:***   "Yes, but if I had done that, it would have been just as disastrous because. . ."

What to say   Being argumentative won't help. Accept the criticism.

> ***Lee:***   "Thanks, Boss, that's certainly another way to look at it."

Be glad your boss cares enough to show you a better way.

Sell Your Ideas

Keep your finger on the company pulse. Use your antennae to spot subjects that are in the air. Think about where the company is probably heading. Analyze recent statements by the CEO so that you can zero in and relate your work to company priorities.

Relating your proposal to company goals

As long as you can tie your idea to stated objectives, go ahead and present it. To have the head honchos see you as an idea person is even more important than having your idea accepted. Just remember that the boss is only interested in achieving the objectives defined for the company.

> **TIP:** You can trigger innovative thoughts. As you read newspapers, magazines, books, and journals, or listen to TV and radio, glean ideas from the media that you can adapt to fit your needs. For instance, you can reword an appeal in a video commercial to enhance your board room presentation. If you borrow directly, credit the source.

Strategy Your objective is to come up with new ways to meet current needs. Demonstrate the value of your proposal. Document data to back up your estimates. Specify projected benefits to the company.

Mona was in stiff competition to get funds allocated for her proposal. I told her to think as though she were the persons doing the allocating. Why does spending money on her project get them closer to where they want to go? How?

What to say Forthright, factually, and unemotionally Mona presented a complete picture including anticipating obstacles.

> *Mona:* "We'll be able to save $10,000 and eliminate 120 work hours while creating good will for the company. I do foresee running into a little difficulty with training, however that can be handled by. . . I've prepared and attached a proposed budget for your consideration."

Stand in the top executives' shoes. Talk their language and give them all the information they need to make an objective decision.

How to submit your plan without an invitation

In companies where departments are invited to submit program improvement requests prior to budget hearings, enterprising employees submit unasked-for proposals whenever they've developed their thoughts.

> **TIP:** Test the water before you dive in. Don't announce prematurely what you're working on. At this point you don't want to be encouraged or discouraged, you're after the facts.

Strategy Your objective is to sell your idea yourself and not have it interpreted by someone who can't do it justice. You can also team up with someone as knowledgeable and enthusiastic and preferably with more clout.

Oscar was convinced his plan would increase production, improve morale, save time, and cut costs—everything top management could ask for. His complete proposal acknowledged problems as well as benefits. He reasoned how the company would lose out if the idea was not accepted. His boss seemed to like it, but was non-committal.

What to say I suggested that Oscar explain the plan at the next level instead of having his boss do it.

> ***Oscar:*** "Boss, I know you will want to talk this over with the executive committee. Would it be possible for me to be with you when you do?"
>
> ***Boss:*** "That's a good idea. You can explain it better than I can and answer their questions."

When you can present your plan better, try to do it yourself and avoid the middleman.

Giving more clout to your suggestion

A few additional pointers:

1. *Find the person your boss most respects and listens to*

> "Frank, I'd like to ask your advice about an idea I think could help us with. . ."

2. *Get guidance.* Follow suggestions exactly. Try to make this person your mentor who'll carry the ball. You'll get your credit soon enough.

> "I'm glad you see potential. How do you suggest I proceed?"

3. *Call on those you've helped in the past.* They know they owe you one.

> "Wanda, would you look over this proposal coming up for discussion and let me know if you can support it? Thanks. I really need your support."

Planting the seed in your boss's mind

You plowed the ground and planted the seed of an idea. It often takes three months to grow. Sure enough, three months later, the boss comes in very excited. ("Gee, a great idea popped into my head while I was driving to work. . .")

TIP: It's great if the boss subconsciously adopted your idea as his own. You know your thinking is on target.

Strategy Your objective is to win approval for something important. Help your office move in a positive direction and you'll eventually get credit for it.

Jody wanted her boss to be receptive to the nucleus of an idea without waiting three months for the idea to germinate.

What to say Here's a faster approach.

Jody: "Boss, I got this idea from something you said at the meeting. . ."

"As you suggested the other day, Boss, I have a little outline on how we can. . ."

"Boss, as a follow-up to our discussion this morning, it occurred to me that. . ."

Without acknowledging it as your idea, the boss subconsciously knows it is and forms a favorable impression of you.

* * *

To impress your boss, stop being part of the herd and be heard. Sell yourself beyond job performance. Consider your appearance, manner of speech, attitude, energy, and innovations when talking to your boss.

CHAPTER 5

$$\Large(\qquad\qquad)$$

Setting the Stage to Ask for a Raise

QUIZ #5. ARE YOU PREPARED TO ASK FOR AN INCREASE?

Check the alternative you'd be more apt to choose. An interpretation of your choices follows.

1. You want the boss to be aware of all that you're doing,

    (a) but you do nothing for fear you'll appear pushy.

    (b) unrequested, you send him a copy of all but your routine work.

2. You see only two alternatives, both undesirable. You

    (a) weigh them again to choose the less objectionable.

    (b) you re-examine the dilemma and try to expand your options.

3. You and a cohort have had a running feud, and you

    (a) counter her distortions with some mud of your own.

    (b) suggest being civil to each other lest you both get fired.

4. The office grapevine is often a tip-off of what is to come. You

      (a) obviously want no part of office "gossip."

      (b) feed the grapevine information about your work.

5. You would like to get legitimate personal publicity, but all your work products are team efforts. Therefore, you

      (a) cannot get individual credit.

      (b) become expert in one aspect of your field to earn recognition.

6. To impress the boss, you do extra curricular work,

      (a) volunteering for everything the boss mentions.

      (b) limited to the boss's pet projects.

7. Your job title doesn't describe your tasks. You

      (a) accept this, content to constantly explain your role.

      (b) risk annointing yourself with a more descriptive working title.

8. Before asking the boss for a raise, you

      (a) tell how hard you work and why you need the money.

      (b) list your major achievements during the past year.

9. You base how much of a raise you ask for on

      (a) how much you actually need

      (b) your research of your job's national and local pay range.

10. Their counteroffer is much less than you can earn elsewhere. You

      (a) accept it to save yourself the trouble of moving on.

      (b) continue negotiating, not accepting less than a pre-decided minimum salary.

Interpretation

If most of your answers are a's, you take the easy way out. Your focus is limited—you don't see beyond the ways in which *you* are affected. Because of this narrow vision, sometimes you fail to appreciate your worth to others and therefore don't try to convince them how good you really are.

If most of your answers are b's, you have an assertive but acceptable manner. You are practical and base your actions on how you and everyone else involved would be affected. You plan tactical ways to advance your career.

HOW TO LAY THE GROUNDWORK BEFORE ASKING FOR A RAISE

It is not working hard that propels you upward or gets you a raise, but working hard on whatever the boss thinks is important. Reinforce the good impressions you make by spinning a web of support. Others give this to you gladly if you feed in information effectively and if you're a team player who pitches in when needed before you are even asked.

Although you are sure you deserve a raise, before you go rushing into the boss's office, be certain you have laid a solid foundation by

- Attaining a good reputation
- Using office politics
- Meshing your goals with company goals

Attaining a Good Reputation

The boss wants to know that you're consistent and steady. You impress the boss by doing a little more than you have to. Maintain your own professional standards and refuse to turn in sloppy work, either produced by you or your subordinates, because the assumption is that messy work means a messy mind.

Informing the boss that your work is consistently good

In the entertainment field, you remember the actor's last role; in sports, the player's last game. In business, your boss remembers your last assignment. Frankly, you can't survive on past triumphs. You're only as good as your last effort or, as some wag observed, the difference between a halo and a noose is eleven inches. Therefore, when you do something well, you want to be certain to inform your boss about it.

> **TIP:** When you can't talk to your boss, attach a brief hand-written note to your report. ("I know this is something that interests you—note last paragraph, page 2.") By frequently telling your boss the status of your tasks, you enable your boss to be accountable when asked how things are going in your division. You create a reflex action—the boss associates your name with accomplishment.

Strategy   Your objective is to find some way to keep your boss apprised of your good work.

(1)   Relate your work to the boss's goals.

(2)   Veil your part beneath a compliment to the effort of your team.

Hilde sends her boss copies of all nonroutine matters, but wanted to know how she could be sure he reads any of it and knows of her nice work.

What to say   In reporting to your boss, there are three words to remember: enthusiasm, modesty, and brevity.

> **Hilde:**   "Boss, I know you'll be pleased to hear the meeting went well. We had good teamwork and the association appeared genuinely receptive to the ideas we suggested."

Hilde can paste another gold star on her chart. What she did well reflects well upon the whole company. She can afford to be generous in praising her entire group since she's the one who molded a few individuals into an effective team.

Getting unsolicited commendations

Being able to move quickly and decisively without holding up your peers and meeting your deadlines are among the best ways to get them spouting spontaneous, unsolicited commendations about you to your boss.

> **TIP:** Vital information sent through interoffice mail can get buried in an In Basket. It is better to personally hand deliver your memos or send a dependable messenger.

Strategy   Your objective is to follow the Golden Rule when dealing with colleagues. Be considerate of the time and effort your peers expend and they will show you more consideration. This also will result in nice reports about you getting back to your boss.

At 10:00 A.M. Margie called Sherrie for some attendance figures she needed that afternoon. Sherrie assured her she'd have them before lunch, but then ran into a problem.

What to say   After promising something for a specific time, call back immediately:

> **Sherrie:**   "Margie, getting those figures you want will take longer than I thought. Is 2:00 P.M. too late to get them to you?"

Acting responsibly earns you a good reputation.

Volunteering before you're asked shows you're a team player

Consider exchanging a little bit of freedom for a little bit more security. Give up a little of your time to get a little better reception. By joining whatever is happening around the office, *gladly* doing more than you have to, you cause the word to spread that you're a member of the club.

TIP: Consider it an opportunity when you have the chance to help someone. You never know how or when you will be repaid. Helping someone now is one way to pay back people who helped you before. Just don't go overboard and volunteer for everything without finishing your own work or your boss may conclude you lack both organizational skills and the judgment to decide what's important.

Strategy   Your objective is to demonstrate to the boss that you're always available to help the department. Anticipate what's needed and volunteer to do it before the boss requests it.

Shelly has been studying her boss's list of priorities and she doesn't have to be nudged to accept any assignment. Color her reliable. But more than that, she's learned to foresee what her boss wants done—sometimes before Melissa, her boss, does.

What to say   In the following exchange, note how Shelly stepped up and volunteered before she was asked.

> **Melissa:** "Shelly, the top brass are making noises about reducing the operating costs of each department by ten percent. If we're forced to take an across-the-board cut, how will services in your division be affected?"
>
> **Shelly:** "We're operating pretty close to the bone, but I know how important it is to maintain our current level of services. Why don't I work up a few alternatives for you to consider. I'll have them for you in the morning."

Being a team player also means going beyond what you and your boss need and seeing what might help your colleagues and your department. For instance, prepare and circulate a succinct report on accomplishments or information exchanged at out-of-office meetings and conferences you attend. Also volunteer to report briefly at the next staff meeting.

Using Office Politics

If you want to get ahead, hang this sign on your wall as a constant reminder: "Only Make Friends." You can't afford any enemies. From your clerk to your CEO, treat each person with respect. And treat everyone alike. In *Pygmalion* (adapted as *My Fair Lady*), George Bernard Shaw expressed it like this: "The great secret, Eliza, is not having bad manners or good manners or any other particular sort of manners, but having the same manner for all human souls."

Mending fences before it's too late

Professionals know that vilifying anyone, even the most obnoxious, is not an option. There are precise and proper ways to deal with incompetence and more effective ways to handle dirty dealing. Name calling isn't one of them. Once you get a negative reputation, it will take months of controlling your every action to try to reverse it and you may not succeed.

TIP: You needn't become buddies with a former enemy. You should try to bury the hatchet someplace besides each other's backs. Getting along with colleagues is a vital skill when you're being considered for advancement.

Strategy Your objective is to patch up any hard feelings that may exist between you and a colleague. Take the first step, explaining that it is mutually beneficial to become friends again and not risk a bad reputation.

Neva and Wilbur have had an ongoing argument about office procedure. Neva believes Wilbur is out to undercut her at every corner and she may be right. She complained to some of his staff who seemed to sympathize with her plight, but they went right back and reported to Wilbur that Neva was saying nasty things about him.

What to say This situation can only fester into full-scale warfare. It's not worth it. I suggested that Neva tie a handkerchief on a ruler, wave her little white flag at the door to Wilbur's office, smile, and ask to discuss it.

> **Neva:** "Wilbur, how about calling a truce? Let's sit down and talk about our problem."
>
> **Wilbur:** "Ok, Neva, I think this *is* getting out of hand."

Wilbur welcomed the opportunity because, as Neva learned later, he had gone to the boss with the problem. But he miscalculated. Their mutual boss goes berserk when she hears about personal feuds and told Wilbur to straighten it out or he and Neva would both be gone.

How to use gossip for your advantage

You can't avoid office politics or keep out of it. Just being in the office makes you involved. Others will talk about you because it's the nature of the group to discuss the players. So you might as well give them something positive to pick up from your casual remarks than leaving them to their own conclusions.

> **TIP:** Use the grapevine. Unless you read tea leaves, you never know who says what to whom about you, so be friends with everyone. A promotion doesn't always go to the most qualified, it may go to the most politically adept.

Strategy   Your objective is to manage the information about you that's fed through the grapevine. Casually mention what you want passed along to anyone who might spread the word to your boss.

Oliver's supervisor, who was asked to draft a speech for the boss, turned in Oliver's work as his own. The boss loved it. Now Oliver wants the boss to know that it was he who wrote the speech and that he's capable of pulling together good information quickly. How could he do this without disparaging his supervisor?

What to say   We decided the safest route was through the boss's assistant.

> *Oliver:*   "My fingers ache from all that research I did preparing the speech the boss is giving this afternoon. But I know he's going to do a great job. He has such charisma..."

The assistant was quick to inform the boss that it was Oliver who had actually written the speech. For the next talk, the boss asked the supervisor to delegate the assignment to Oliver.

Listening and speaking up when needed

Besides feeding information into the grapevine, you have to gently pull information out. While you have your nose to the grindstone, keep your ears to the ground. Listen to what's going on around you and you'll find many opportunities to be helpful or even save the day.

> **TIP:** Do a small favor and win a friend. Be quick to pick up the cue when you hear a colleague needs a helping hand. At that moment a minor problem seems enormous. Come to the rescue. ("I've pulled emergency duty this weekend and it's my wife's birthday. She's going to have a fit!") You offer to exchange weekends. No big sacrifice for you, but you've won eternal gratitude.

Strategy Your objective is to keep alert and quickly sift through all the talk surrounding you. Sort the information you hear into three categories—for immediate use, for later use, and for the disposal.

Kevin heard Joy predicting to anyone who'd listen that a new procedure would prove defective.

> **Joy:** "Just you wait. When they start with that new 30-day requirement, there'll be an epidemic of flu excuses in this office."

What to say Reading the storm signals, Kevin intervened by offering the boss a positive suggestion.

> **Kevin:** "Boss, to avoid a morale problem, we may need to do a better job of explaining the new 30-day regulation. Why don't we get a small committee to suggest how to do this? Maybe Joy would be a good one to chair it?"

Kevin helped avert a potentially serious problem by listening and speaking up.

Helping your mentor sound better

Mentors are in the position to help you develop your skills, make the right contacts, and generally guide you in your upward climb. Quite often they want to help simply because they like you. Or it may be their way of reciprocating for assistance they received on the way up.

The best mentor may be your own boss, but caring goes both ways. Anticipate the boss's problems, offer solutions, and double-check your facts. Suggest ideas that make the boss look and sound better. Then you feel at ease asking the boss for advice and guidance.

Sharing resources and solutions with your personal network

While networking often applies outside your office where members attend professional or trade meetings to share solutions for the same kinds of problems, there is also networking, both formal and unorganized, within your office. It boils down to being a friend and, in return, having a friend, and showing sincere interest and pleasure when your friend succeed. Then your colleagues will trust you and listen to what you say. Don't keep your career ambitions a secret from them if there is any way they can assist you. Seek their advice. Those who are in a position to do so will put in the right word where it counts.

> **TIP:** Keep a contact file. Get a small alphabetical index card file to record names, addresses, phone numbers, and comments about contacts you've made or want to develop.

Proclaiming yourself a more fitting title

Drama students have it drummed into their heads that there are no small parts, only small actors. It's the same way with any role in your company. The job grows to the limits of your insight and imagination. Be careful not to upstage anyone and the rest of the crew will be glad to see your part become as big as you can make it. If your job classification is meaningless even to those within your organization, try anointing yourself with a new *working* title.

> **TIP:** Your opportunity may come as a soft tap instead of a loud knock. Grab the chance to do extra work if that lets you learn a new skill you've been wanting to master. Most supervisors are pleased when their subordinates take initiative.

Strategy Your objective is to make the most of your job and to see its potential as a stepping stone. Study your operation for better, faster, cheaper, more effective ways to do anything related to your job.

Doug, a program analyst in the Grants Administration Section, decided to call himself "Assistant to the Grants Administrator" because this better described his actual work.

What to say When his boss questioned the new title on the correspondence, he explained:

Doug: "Boss, most people don't understand what a program analyst does. I did this to clear up the confusion over how I could be of service to those contacting the office. Is that all right with you?"

Of course he would have backed off if the boss objected. The following year Doug shortened the title to "Assistant Grants Administrator." Even though Doug crowned himself (and this has nothing to do with the salary negotiation other than more accurately describing what he really does) everyone in the company began to think of Doug as having been promoted. When you sense the time is right to take the initiative, act on it.

Meshing Your Goals with Company Goals

Before asking for a raise, link your personal objectives with the specific company needs you can best meet. Listen carefully when your boss talks, observe which projects the boss authorizes expenditures for, or where extra staff and other movable resources are concentrated. If you are going to be paid more by the company, you have to give the company something it particularly wants in the way that it wants it. Working painstakingly is not enough to merit a raise unless you are spending your time on the boss's priorities.

Matching the boss's style when presenting your case

Bosses have their own way of handling situations. Study your boss's style so that you can present your case in a manner the boss will accept. Some pick apart every possibility, methodically sorting facts before choosing. Others go for the desired result:

> "Spare me the analysis and details. I only want to discuss general strategy."

Some are impatient to get going:

> "Look we already know what works. Enough talk. I want action."

Some bosses are synthesizers. They ask a few people on the same team to prepare the exact same report, each not knowing the others are doing it. Hearing them out together is not meant to embarrass anyone but to assemble the pieces of each report closest to what the boss is looking for.

Determine your boss's style so that you'll know how much to include or leave out of your talk.

Acknowledging the boss's priorities

Before you prepare your pitch, understand the company's point of view. It really doesn't matter that you can't manage on your present salary, or your daughter needs an operation, or your old car keeps breaking down and you must get some other transportation. The main obligation of the boss, a nice person who'd like to help, is not to you but the company. The only questions from the top are:

1: "Why do you think you're worth more to us than we are now paying you?"

2: "How does investing in you benefit the company?"

Asking for more money can be intimidating. Being rejected is worse. To overcome this fear, you have to be convinced your work is worth more.

If it's been a thorn in your side waiting for the raise you feel should be given you without your even asking for it, your resentment will affect your work. Deal with this by preparing a presentation that tells the boss what the boss needs to know.

Preparing your pitch

Before you ask for a raise, determine what's going on in your company and in your job market, and how much you think your work is worth. Can your company afford the raise? Must requests be in at set times such as three months before final budget? Will your cohorts also be asking for a raise? What is the going pay range for your type of job nationally and locally?

> **TIP:** After gathering national and local data, compile a one-page Pay Rate Chart on your type work. This, together with a crisp report of your Achievement Highlights over the past year, gives you something concrete to discuss with your boss.

Strategy Your objective is to be persuasive, to sound confident, business-like, and believable.

  (1) Based on national and local data, decide in advance the minimum salary you'll accept, the minimum amount you feel you're worth and can earn elsewhere.

  (2) List recent accomplishments—specific ways you helped cut costs, increase sales, and so on.

Ava, an executive assistant, has been at the same job nine years, always getting excellent ratings. She just learned at a national conference that others doing the same kind of work make considerably more money and she's understandably upset. We developed a plan of action:

  (1) To learn the going pay range for her particular job, she obtained figures from her professional association and from her company's personnel department. She learned the pay scale for jobs similar to hers.

  (2) To see what's currently available locally, she combed the newspaper want ads and called a few employment agencies.

  (3) To examine the possibility of carving a new position for herself with a bigger salary, she listed additional duties assumed this year without a raise, analyzing how important these are to her boss.

To speak to her boss with conviction, Ava had to appear assertive. She had to study her options:

  • Keep working here if the minimum raise is refused. Will her pride let her work for less?

  • Quit if she doesn't get a salary increase. Are there other employers waiting for her in the wings?

  • Keep working here if the raise is refused while secretly seeking other employment. Does she depend on uninterrupted income?

What to say Ava rehearsed her talk with a close colleague, trying to think the way their boss does and trying to anticipate every possible question and response.

  Ava: "He'll say, it's company policy to give raises only when...and I'll say, but isn't it also company policy to acknowledge..."

Friend: "I agree your work is worth another $5,000, however $2,000 is the absolute limit. . ."

Ava: "Since we agree my work is worth another $5,000, surely you'll understand that a $2,000 increase is not sufficient. Why don't we split the difference at $3,500?"

Friend: "If I give you a raise, it'll have a domino effect we can't afford."

Ava: "I know you can't afford across-the-board raises, but don't you want to motivate the special people like me who get you the results you want?"

Friend: "Ava, your work is very good, but there's no room now for you to advance."

Ava: "I don't mind waiting a while to advance if we can discuss additional fringe benefits and eliminating weekend work."

Delivering your request for a raise

Here are a few reminders:

(1) *Ask your boss for a few uninterrupted minutes.* You want to be sure your timing is right.
(2) *Talk in a strong voice.* Keep calm, unemotional, no whining or crying. Remember to be pleasant and conversational.
(3) *Start with a friendly greeting.* Be brief and get right to the point.

> "Boss, I've come here today to talk to you about my raise."

Because you've practiced, you can sound enthusiastic although your heart does flip-flops. It's acceptable to glance at your notes, but keep looking the boss in the eye. Watch the eyes and other types of body language. The boss slowly wiping his eyeglasses, for example, is probably thinking about the point you just made—keep still a moment. Drumming fingers on the table or playing with a key ring indicates impatience—go to the next item.

Extracting valuable lessons from the boss's comments

Whatever the result of your request, you've alerted the boss that you want to move up and you will be watched more closely.

If you got the full raise, congratulations! If you negotiated a compromise you can live with, such as extra benefits, that's great too. If the rejection had nothing to do with you personally ("I'm sorry, you're already at the top step in your classification") then do what you can, such as immediately working on getting reclassified.

If, however, you were turned down without good reason, don't slam the door on the way out. Just walk away without bluffing or threatening to quit and say,

> "Thanks for your time." or
>
> "I understand you can't do anything now. I'll think about what you said and get back to you."

TIP: It may definitely be to your advantage to look for another job, but keep that your secret for a while. If you slam the door at this time, how are you going to open it again to ask for a reference in three weeks when you're ready to give notice?

Strategy Your objective, besides the raise, was to learn as much as you could about where you stand. Note the boss's responses so that you can consider the options when you get back to your desk.

Neelie was disheartened because her boss Jay had just rejected her request for a raise. In his doing so, however, she learned quite a bit of helpful information. The boss disclosed areas in which she should improve.

What to say Neelie accepted the criticism and restated it in a positive way.

> **Jay:** "You're doing more than your job. You're trying to do someone else's job, too."

Neelie: "I admit I try to be helpful. I'll be back in three months to prove to you I've toned down."

If you understand why the raise could not be given you now, you can concentrate on making an indelible impression for next time. You have incentive to work even harder, with belief in yourself that next time your request will be granted.

* * *

In essence, your getting a raise is not based on your needs or even on the amount of work you do or how well you do it. The decision hinges on your ability to communicate to the decision-maker how valuable you are in helping your company achieve its desired results. If you are perceived as a rising star, others will want to help you.

PART TWO

What to Say to the People You Work With

CHAPTER 6

Sending the Right Message to Vexing Colleagues

If you were faced with the following situations, which choice best describes your behavior? An interpretation of your choices follows.

1.   When your cohorts try to get your goat, do you

   (a) tell them it's not funny and to stop the nonsense?
   (b) get so mad that you are unable to say anything?
   (c) try to kid them back or smile and remain silent?

2.   A fellow worker cleverly disguises the pot shots she takes at you. Do you

   (a) first try to figure out why she's being critical?
   (b) pretend to be amused?
   (c) strike back with even more cutting remarks?

3.   If your teammate keeps trying to tear you down in front of the others, would you

   (a) ask his advice, allowing him to feel important?
   (b) confront him publicly to let everybody know what he's up to?

93

(c) avoid contact with him as much as you possibly can?

4. You've run up against the coercive bully. Do you

   (a) do whatever she wants in order not to make waves?
   (b) call her bluff by standing up and refusing her dictates?
   (c) try to reason with her?

5. When you tangle with aggressive, overwhelming bulldozers, do you

   (a) do it their way, feeling it's easier than holding your own?
   (b) fight back, telling the bulldozers where they're wrong?
   (c) avoid a head-on collision by quietly remaining firm?

6. You got together on a joint proposal, but your friends left you standing alone in advocating passage. Do you

   (a) attack them and expose their cowardice in front of the gang?
   (b) suffer silently and vow never to team up with anyone else again?
   (c) suffer silently, and vow that next time there'll be a signed joint proposal, jointly presented?

7. When you hear a rumor around the office that could have serious consequences, do you

   (a) refuse to act on it until you've verified the facts?
   (b) enjoy being one of the first who can spread the news?
   (c) dismiss it, regardless of the facts?

8. You need advice on a continuing basis from a peer who responds in one-word answers. Do you

   (a) confront him, accusing him of being uncooperative?
   (b) get your information from a less satisfactory source?
   (c) ask him more specific questions?

9. Your colleague at the next desk is a phony know-it-all who wastes your time. You can't avoid her. Do you

   (a) press her for details that will reveal her phoniness?

(b) give her the stony-stare silent treatment?

(c) hear her out, but don't comment on her advice?

10. When some people ask impertinent questions, or make impertinent requests, do you

(a) explain why you can't comply?

(b) comply, hating yourself for it?

(c) simply refuse, refraining from any explanation?

11. A co-worker is trying to manipulate you into bailing him out of a problem he should handle himself. Do you

(a) feel sorry for him and do what he asks?

(b) tell him to get lost?

(c) refuse to do it but offer to help him prepare?

12. In your office, collections for presents and parties have become epidemic. Do you

(a) bark at the hat-passers, telling them you're fed up?

(b) help establish office policy to control plate-passing?

(c) shrug it off and contribute to everything whether you want to or not?

Interpretation

Most of your answers will fall into one of three groups:

GROUP I: 1a, 2c, 3b, 4c, 5b, 6a, 7b, 8a, 9b, 10a, 11b, 12a.
GROUP II: 1b, 2b, 3c, 4a, 5a, 6b, 7c, 8b, 9c, 10b, 11a, 12c.
GROUP III: 1c, 2a, 3a, 4b, 5c, 6c, 7a, 8c, 9a, 10c, 11c, 12b.

If you are mostly GROUP I, you're not going to let anyone get away with anything. However, these responses are not winning you friends or influencing colleagues. Temper your anger; mix a little honey with the vinegar. You are going to need your peers on the way up. Try harder to understand their needs as well as your own.

If you are mostly GROUP II, you're not being really honest with yourself by pretending it doesn't bother you when others bully or manipulate you. Furthermore, by not correcting the problem, you are perpetuating it. Practice stating your position more frequently and you will gain new self-respect as well as more respect from your fellow workers.

If you are mostly GROUP III, you've got your eye on the future. You usually get along well with all types, including problem people who could otherwise toss a monkey wrench into your career-climbing path. With comments that are assertive but not hostile, you hold your own without being offensive. People appreciate knowing where they stand with you.

HOW TO CONFRONT THE AFFRONTERS

The reality is that there's at least one goat-getter in every office. They have no more authority than you have, but somehow they manage to get a measure of control over you. And there you are treating them with kid gloves while they fleece you out of your self respect.

You can't change these goat-getters, bullies, manipulators, and mavins. That's how they are. Trying to alter their behavior wastes your time and energy. More importantly, that's not getting the result you're after. So, even if their antics get under your skin, don't say anything rash to your colleagues.

Concentrate instead on what you can change. You can't change them, but you can alter how you speak to them and thereby get on top of sticky situations.

In this chapter, we'll look at positive logical action to curb your natural negative emotional reaction to peers who get your goat. First, you'll shift the focus to the outcome you're seeking, and then you'll learn the script that can make it happen as we examine

- Bullish responses to bullies
- Trusty put-downs when you're being used
- Pointed queries for the know-it-all

Bullish Responses to Bullies

Their overbearing insistence to have things done their way is infuriating. After going only one round of verbal abuse with a bully, you feel punched out, drained of your fighting spirit. When they huff and puff trying to blow your house down, stop treating these offenders so tenderly. Put on velvet gloves over an iron fist and fight back.

How to verbally counterpunch your intimidators

No matter what kind of intimidator is browbeating you, the vital guideline to remember is: *Stand up to the bully*. This doesn't mean a shouting match or name-calling, but rather quietly hold your own, state your view, or correct misinformation or misconceptions. If you kowtow to an abuser, it's woo today, woe tomorrow. You have to stand up for yourself to gain everyone's respect—the aggressor's, the on-watchers, and most important, your own.

TIP: Be still for a couple of minutes and let the bully land those cutting remarks without your interrupting. Force yourself to wear a pleasant "I know something you don't know" expression while you prepare your response. Now get in the ring, even if your bully hasn't stopped jabbing.

Strategy Keep your cool and state your case calmly, unemotionally, and resolutely rather than criticizing your opponents with a frontal attack. Responding with anger would only infuriate them. And, in some cases, they'd seek revenge forever and you'd be left with a lifetime enemy.

This tactic helped Perry, a project director, who on his own initiative had prepared an alternative budget procedure to present at the next management meeting. He told me he felt uneasy knowing that Leon, another project director, would be there.

Leon believes with fanatic fervor that his way is the only way. Simply debating the issue can't feed his need to feel superior, he has to tear his victim to shreds with a personal attack. In their last encounter, Leon made Perry appear incompetent by breaking into Perry's talk and running over him like a bulldozer.

What to say Predictably, Leon interrupted at the management meeting, about halfway through Perry's presentation. But this time Perry was prepared to regain control. Note how strongly and firmly, yet quietly and courteously, Perry stood up to the bully during this exchange at the meeting. The goal was to finish the presentation. To do so, Perry wisely put a lid on his agitation and fear as he flagged down the bulldozer and steered clear of a head-on collision.

>*Leon:* "You know, team, that's really a ridiculous proposition. It's full of flaws because Perry is ignorant of the economic principles involved. Let's get on with more important business."
>
>*Perry:* "Look, Leon, I understand that so far you don't like my plan. Really, that's OK, even though I don't agree. I feel the plan meets an urgent need to streamline our operation. However, you may be right. After I finish explaining it, we can all decide if it should be adopted, adapted, or dumped. Now, as I was saying..."

Answering co-workers who block your ideas

Sometimes attackers simply hunger for more recognition and try to get it by blocking their colleagues. Unlike Leon who reacts out of the passionate conviction that he's infallible, these blockers have no such belief. To them, the more holes they can punch in your ideas, the bigger and better they think they'll appear.

TIP: Wanting to clobber a critic is a natural impulse, but you've more to gain using your brain. Keep reminding yourself that your aim is to get their support.

Strategy Acknowledge the blocker's skill by asking his or her advice. "You've had good results handling xyz, what do you suggest?" This is particularly important when talking to people like Beverly. She's a pulley-system operator, following the "if I can push you down, I'll automatically move up" philosophy. April felt hurt and frustrated after Beverly tackled her for making a suggestion to the group.

>*Beverly:* "That's a pretty stupid idea, April. It can't possibly work. You haven't allowed nearly enough time to..."

What to say April needed a way to appear innovative now and also gain the support she'd require later. Since the boss seemed to listen carefully whenever Beverly spoke, one apparent answer was to ask Beverly for advice. This April could do and still maintain her self-assurance. The next time before taking the idea to the group, April brought it to Bev.

> *April:* "What do you think about this, Beverly? I know you're the in-house authority on interpreting federal regs; I'd like your opinion."

So basic and so simple, and yet the words worked like magic. Beverly actually shared some thoughts with April without an audience present because April acknowledged Beverly's past successes. April could then decide if she wanted to modify her idea with Beverly's suggestions—giving credit, of course, for the help. If April decided not to use them, at least she'd know what to expect at the meeting and be prepared to counter Beverly's arguments.

How to needle the needlers and still look good

Needling bullies are more subtle than brash bullies. Their pointed, provoking teasing may or may not be intentionally cruel, but they use their greater wit or quick thinking to intimidate their peers. Needlers make jokes at your expense. Quite often, what they present as humor is in reality a cover-up for their criticism or malicious insinuations.

TIP: In dealing with needlers, shift the object of their objection away from you and toward something impersonal, such as a policy or a procedure. For example, when a needler belittles you for taking so much time to write up a new regulation, don't try to defend yourself for taking the amount of time you need. Instead, start discussing the regulation itself.

Strategy Needle the needlers until they get the point. Look around and listen carefully—you're not the only target. Talk to the others individually about ganging up on the needler. He will soon realize that he's not accomplishing very much.

Cliff wanted to know how to stop a sniper from taking pot shots at him. He explained that Donald wouldn't risk open warfare, but encases his sharp remarks in a joke or a laugh, and has managed to get a rise out of most of the staff. Don's humorous jabs are actually piercing, painfully embarrassing, public ridicule. For instance, in front of others Donald would goad him with, "Cliff, don't give up. If you work on this for another seven years, you may get it right. Ha ha."

What to say Having talked to Donald's other victims, Cliff was ready the next time Donald started to needle him. Observe how Cliff forced Donald out in the open, and invited the others to join in.

> *Cliff:* "Donald, did you mean that as a dig?" (and without a pause, continuing to the entire group) "Did you hear what I heard?"
>
> *Arlene:* "Donald, it would help us if you'd make your criticism clear."
>
> *Warren:* "Don, apparently this is easy for you. But please explain your explanation."
>
> *Gil:* "Don, please clarify that clarification."

When you're the only one they tease

For some people joking is difficult. Not everyone can be a stand-up comic, especially if one is hurt too deeply by the clowns to find anything laughable in their jests. People use quasi humor (their remarks resemble humor but aren't really funny) to satisfy their own needs and don't realize—or care about—the pain or embarrassment they inflict. The victims they choose are those who react the most, preferably with indignant anger.

> **TIP:** Whenever you can do it, kid the person who's getting your goat. "That's a half-baked excuse." "On the contrary, I thought it was well-done."

Strategy Take away their fun and they'll stop gunning you.

Stu's problem was that everyone was always teasing or playing tricks, but only on him. Stu's puritanical background made him cringe whenever his colleagues derived pleasure from joking and enjoying more than the intellectual aspect of work. They started a rumor that Stu lacked a sense of humor, and they couldn't resist the temptation to get him to unbend.

One day at a working lunch, for instance, Stu spilt tomato soup on his tie and Arthur, the office clown, suggested that Stu should sit on the table and eat off the chair. Stu turned as red as the stain.

What to say   Straight-laced Stu couldn't joke back, but we agreed that he would force himself to smile as he remained silent. Gradually, he relaxed a bit and they stopped saying that Stu was a snob. Particularly after he started going with them once in a while for morning coffee.

When someone gives you a left-handed compliment

Another type of needler gives back-handed compliments. They pull you closer by saying something nice and then take you by surprise when they slap you down. "That was a kind act—coming from you."

There's a two-step routine for replying to a left-handed compliment that will put you in control.

(1) graciously accept the legitimate part.

(2) assume your most erect posture and toss back the rest of the statement with a polite contradiction or correction.

Here's how this worked for Bobbie. Never sure how to react to Millicent's disguised digs, Bobbie had been swallowing hard and practically gagging on a thank you. She had to stop buying into Millicent's put downs.

What to say   We practiced several variations of accepting the compliment while challenging the insult.

> ***Millicent:***   "That's good work, Bobbie, especially for someone who's new."
>
> ***Bobbie:***   "Thank you, Millicent. I'm glad you like it. Although I haven't been with this company very long, I did have several years experience doing this work before I came here."

Trusty Put-downs When You Are Being Used

Some co-workers take advantage of the good nature of their peers and use them for their own advantage. They connive to get their hooks into you and let you dangle as they pull the puppet strings. Unwittingly or begrudgingly, you do their deeds.

When colleagues take advantage of you

Do you sometimes feel exploited or that you're being used to further someone else's ambitions? The only way your peers can impose upon you is for you to let them step all over you.

TIP: If you don't want to become their doormat, pull the rug out from under the imposers.

Strategy   Say as little as possible, but make it clear that you refuse to be used. State your refusal matter-of-factly, leaving no room for debate. Don't worry about hurting their feelings. The insensitive, by definition, have no feelings to hurt. There's no need to give a reason when you refuse to answer an impertinent personal question or request.

That was the lesson Suzie had to learn. She kept doing favors for Marlene that were never returned. Typically, every time Marlene decided to take a two-hour lunch, she'd tell Suzie to handle her clients who phoned in. Suzie didn't mind this until it became a habit. Now she wanted a way out.

What to say   It was much easier than Suzie had anticipated. After a few practice runs, she handled the next encounter with dispatch. She merely rejected the request and said no.

> *Marlene:*   "Suzie, I'm leaving. Catch my phone calls."
>
> *Suzie:*   "I can't do that, Marlene. I've something else scheduled."

Finally, it registered on Marlene's brain that she couldn't take advantage of Suzie anymore.

When your "friends" pump you for information

A more difficult situation was Paul's turning down an old friend from another department who was trying to pry out of him information that should stay within Paul's office. The more Paul hedged, the more David pushed.

What to say   Paul finally realized that David was not his good buddy. If your friend continues to push you after this kind of exchange, that person is not your friend. Protect yourself, like this:

David:	"What's the matter, pal. Don't you trust me?"
Paul:	"Why are you asking me for this, David? What is it you're so concerned about?" (and then, a pleasant refusal) "David, I know that being my dear friend, you would not want to see me get into trouble."

When you are left holding the bag

Some cohorts use others to ensure themselves a safe position. If things go wrong, they're free from the blame leaving you out on that limb while everyone else yells "Timber!"

When you and your colleagues take part in presenting a request or proposal, keep yourself from being set up.

TIP: Make some provision to commit your fellow planners to the proposal before you proceed. The best method is preventive—a communicative safety belt—such as having joint signatures on a report or preparing a joint presentation.

Strategy Have your colleagues agree in writing with the proposal you're presenting. You all take the credit or the blame, and no one becomes the fall guy.

This had never occurred to trusting Ben. He joined forces with Arnie and Jack to concoct what the three agreed was a great battle plan for securing some new equipment. They appointed Ben the spokesman to present the idea. The boss didn't like the plan. Others picked up the cue. Jack and Arnie joined in the attack. Riddled by critical comments from all sides, Ben's idea was shot down. Alone and bewildered, he felt he'd been betrayed.

What to say In recounting the incident to me, Ben was still bristling. You expect opposition, he said, but when your friends cut and run—that's hard to take. Ben needed a clear-the-air confrontation to prevent this from happening again.

Ben:	"Jack, Arnie, I don't appreciate you guys backing off on our proposal. Next time we work together, we'll also submit the plan in writing and you'll sign it."

While the whole episode embarrassed Ben, he learned about the importance of taking precautions to protect himself.

When a peer's friendship is phony

Among common manipulators at the office are the phony friends who butter up their colleagues to gain their own objectives. You may find yourself in this dilemma: Do you do something you think is wrong or do you suffer the consequences of not helping your colleagues?

> **TIP:** When you feel trapped by a phony friend, you are probably more scared than snared. Most likely, you've overestimated your "friend's" power, for if the manipulators wielded that kind of clout, they would not be trying so hard to use you.

It's nice to help colleagues in a difficulty, but you're really not helping them grow up if you shoulder their responsibility. In any case, your objective is to control the outcome.

Strategy Come up with a different scenario than your manipulator suggests. To do this:

(1) Analyze the situation. Is what you're being asked to do your job?
(2) Determine what options are open to the manipulator. What other way can it be handled—ethically?
(3) Decide what you can say to help this person do the right thing, by accepted standards.

Selina thought it was odd that all of a sudden, Donna started asking her to lunch and telling her what a fabulous job she was doing. Instant friendship. After a couple of weeks of flattery, Donna told Selina about a mistake she had made and begged Selina, her "closest friend," to talk to the boss for her. Selina confided to me that she didn't want to talk to the boss, but she was afraid that Donna would get even if she didn't help her. Knowing how Donna put down other colleagues, she feared she was capable of ruining her reputation around the office.

What to say The mistake that had been made was Donna's problem and there was no need for Selina to make it hers. Note how constructively and empathetically Selina was able to turn around a bad situation to everyone's advantage.

> ***Donna:*** "Please, Selina, you're the only one in this whole place I can trust. Please talk to the boss for me."
>
> ***Selina:*** "Donna, that's not what you need. You have to talk to the boss yourself. I'll help you prepare for it so that you'll handle yourself more confidently."

It is possible to maintain your professional integrity and still help out a friend.

When the collection plate comes around again

Every office has a self-appointed deacon who taps the staff for another cause, making those who don't give feel like sinners. In some offices, the money you dish out for the collection plate becomes big bucks that put a huge dent in your wallet.

TIP: When you're asked to participate in something you don't want to, the goal is to control the situation that's out of hand.

Strategy Since most people resent being hounded by plate-passers, bring up the matter for group discussion. This could make you the office hero.

Ted was complaining that Pass-The-Hat Pat was constantly assaulting his cash flow. He didn't even know Sam, but chipped in for the new baby's blanket. He resented paying part of Al's fancy promotion gift, especially when Al never gave him the time of day.

What to say When a simple, unembarrassed refusal is not enough, turn to the group for resolution.

> ***Ted:*** "Sorry, Pat, no."
>
> ***Pat:*** "Why not, Ted?" (plate-passers are awfully pushy)
>
> ***Ted:*** "I can't this time, Pat." (flat, but firm, final tone)

> ***Ted:*** (to the group) "It seems to me that the number of collections lately is getting out of hand. We need to establish a reasonable office policy. An amount we put into the pot every payday for all presents. Or, let each one take care of his own gift."

The others agreed to chip in money once a week for a "present" fund. By confronting an annoying and persistent problem, Ted led the group into working out a reasonable solution.

Pointed Queries for the Know-It-Alls

These co-worker irritants are the connoisseurs who know everything about everything and won't tell you—or who think they know everything. Your hair stands on end after a phony know-it-all flaunts his opinion and cons you into accepting his drivel. Some steer you wrong on important work matters, and some who could steer you right, won't.

How to pry needed information from the clam

Clams are smart colleagues who puzzle you because instead of offering helpful suggestions, they stay silent and appear to be looking down their noses at everyone else's ignorance.

> **TIP:** To get these individuals to talk, avoid posing general questions that let them get away with yes or no answers.

Strategy

(1) Ask them to fill you in on specific points.

(2) Patiently wait for a response.

(3) Repeat this set procedure each time.

Flo needed help in communicating with Calvin. A crowbar couldn't pry out the important information she needed to do her job. How could she get Cal to open up?

What to say Flo had to start with a question that required a little discussion.

> ***Flo:*** "Calvin, how much time should we allow for a complete computer printout?"

Then she had to wait, smiling and silently, for a reply. Though it took a few minutes, she didn't move. She didn't weaken, she didn't speak. Finally, he answered.

> ***Calvin:*** "Well, that depends on a number of variables. The approximate time range would be from. . ."

TIP: After a while you may find that what your clam really wants is more recognition. Start to verbalize your appreciation for his or her knowledge and you'll find the clam gradually opening up.

How to silence misleading mavins

Some peers are so convincing, it's easy to take their advice without question. Possessing a patchwork of facts, they lay claim to being an instant expert on everything. But sometimes, when you follow like sheep you can get sheared as these mavins pull the wool over your eyes.

TIP: Expose phonies for what they are. Check out the mavin's claim and then, in a matter-of-fact manner, present your contradictory but verified information.

Strategy Ask them to interpret their statements and keep pressing them for details on the data they spout.

This was the approach Nick finally used with Edward, a mavin who has absorbed a smattering about any subject you want to discuss. For example, Nick was planning a company picnic in a local park. Edward was emphatic that a permit was needed. Nick wasted two hours on the phone until he was convinced no one ever heard of such a permit. It's not funny being fooled by a phony. Nick came in looking for a way to reveal the void in Edward's gray matter that would leave Ed red-faced in front of the gang.

What to say I reminded Nick that he really wanted a way to keep Edward from wasting his time. Nick practiced questions that would pin down details and render Edward speechless the next time that know-it-all volunteered misleading data.

> *Edward:* "The law requires that you get a permit to hold an outdoor event."
>
> *Nick:* "Edward, where did you hear about such events requiring a permit? What department does this come under? Tell me, which events do and which ones don't come under this order? How far in advance must the permit be obtained?"

Using this technique will quickly silence your office know-it-all.

How to quell a rumor

How do you handle the phony know-it-alls who have all the latest news—and some of it wrong. When do you listen to them? What do you say to idle gossip? What if you ignore an important tipoff?

When a story appears to be personal defamation which is unrelated to work, you can frustrate the gossip with a smiling, "Gee, I really don't know the facts. Why don't you ask (the victim) to fill you in?" When you take away their satisfaction, scandalmongers stop coming back to you. On the other hand, when a juicy tidbit has powderkeg potential, take quick action.

TIP: To quell a rumor, aim to separate truth from fiction. Determine if you are hearing fact, his-say, her-say, or hearsay.

Strategy Trace, then face, the rumor. Check for verification whenever there could be serious consequences at stake for you, your unit or your company.

Pam wanted to know, short of stuffing a gag in Celeste's mouth, how to institute some rumor control. Celeste peddles information in exchange for a little notice. Her reports are distorted, taken out of context, leaving only the parts that interest her. Celeste dwells on the dramatic or embroiders the story to make her role more important.

What to say   Start by grilling the messenger. Then pick up the phone to confirm the information.

> ***Celeste:***   "Pam, did you hear that our downtown branch is closing? And I understand that personnel has to figure out this week how many will be laid off."
>
> ***Pam:***   "Celeste, who said so? Where did you hear this? How reliable is your information? Do you know that's actually going to happen? When?"

Pam learned over the phone, with Celeste still there, that Celeste's story was only partially true. She'd deleted a less exciting essential. Starting next month, the downtown branch will be closing—on Saturdays. Confronted with the facts, Celeste slipped sheepishly away.

You can learn to cope with the vexing, annoying, provoking goat-getters in your office. Forget about locking horns and seeking revenge. Instead, change the way you speak to them. Use what *you* say to gain control over the difficult people you have to deal with.

CHAPTER 7

$$\Big(\qquad\qquad\qquad\Big)$$

Speaking Up and Speaking Out

QUIZ #7. HOW WELL ARE YOU SPEAKING UP TO YOUR PEERS?

If you can't stand up for yourself among your peers, how will you ever stand a chance with your boss? To determine how well you're doing, imagine yourself in the following situations. Choose the one answer for each question that most closely fits you. An interpretation of your choices follows.

1. You often agree to do tasks assigned to co-workers because you

    (a) are too embarrassed to refuse
    (b) don't want to lose their friendship
    (c) know they will help you out when you need them

2. You feel if you refuse a request, your colleague

    (a) might make things difficult for you
    (b) must be made to understand when you can't comply
    (c) will find someone else to do it

3. To refuse habitual imposers, you'd probably

    (a) give three or four excuses why you can't do it

     (b) explain your conflict and ask for a rain check

     (c) say you're sorry that you won't be able to do it

4. By stalling some decisions, you caused a few cohorts to be late with their work. You can solve the problem if you

     (a) apologize to each one you may have inconvenienced

     (b) gather information you need more quickly

     (c) base more decisions on planning from past experience

5. After your colleague was promoted to the job you desperately wanted, you decided

     (a) there is no use trying so hard to get ahead

     (b) to say nothing and wait for another opening to try again

     (c) to ask your boss how to improve your chances next time

6. It's come back to you that the feelings of some of your team members have been hurt by your remarks, and so you'll

     (a) be careful to avoid these people as much as possible

     (b) bite your tongue before saying anything unkind again

     (c) apologize sincerely and quickly for insensitive comments

7. You come in early to finish your report, but a talkative peer sits down at your desk. You

     (a) tolerate the interruption, hoping the peer will soon leave

     (b) hint that you have a lot of work to complete

     (c) smile and escort the peer out, explaining your deadline

8. When you phone colleagues for pertinent information, you resent time wasted on irrelevant matters. You

     (a) can't interrupt their extraneous monologues

     (b) plan to watch the clock more closely

     (c) practice a few polite "hang-up" lines

9. You've heard that getting along with others is a key to success. Consequently, you

(a) worry how your colleagues interpret whatever you say

(b) try to make sure others understand your motivation

(c) realize others are too busy worrying about themselves to analyze everything you say

10. You do your work so well, your supervisor doesn't want you to advance. You know you should ask for help,

(a) but you'll settle for being appreciated

(b) but you don't want to impose on anyone

(c) and turn to some peers who could learn some of your work

Interpretation

If most of your answers are a's, then you hardly speak up. You're afraid of your shadow. You'd rather keep still than ever take a risk and make known your wants. You let fear, anxiety, and insecurity control your reason and lock your lips.

If most of your answers are b's, then you speak up at times. You are basically a gracious person who doesn't want to offend anyone. You know what to say, but don't always do so because you tend to be overly cautious about doing the right thing or being considered nice by your peers.

If most of your answers are c's, you usually speak up. You know when to speak and you do it confidently. You won't accept any guilt that peers may try to lay on you. You don't wait for what you want to come to you, but say what you can to create the opportunity.

HOW TO RELEASE THE WORDS THAT ARE STUCK IN YOUR THROAT

To hold your own in today's job market, competence isn't enough. You have to outshine the others. And there are times, instead of silence being golden and glittering, that remaining silent can tarnish your image. In fact, over the years being mute can cost you a mint.

You've probably been told that if you keep your mouth shut, you can sail along in the same job forever. That's a myth. There's no such guarantee. Among the workers drifting from job to job or drowning in an undertoe of reorganization are those who were afraid to talk lest they rock the boat. So practice speaking out by speaking up to your peers. Remember, you can:

- say no
- resolve problems
- control interruptions
- ask for help

Saying Yes or No—Go One Way or the Other

This country may need a Workaholics Anonymous for those on an organizational toot trying to tote the whole load. Many over-do because they've never mastered the art of saying no. If you are addicted to the indiscriminate "yes," here are words to keep you from falling off the wagon.

How to say no without feeling guilty

Some people have a conscience that works time and a half. They believe they're not carrying their fair share if they don't pitch in and comply with requests from their colleagues each and every time. If you are one of these livewires, practice saying no before you blow a fuse. Admit that the lights won't go off all over the company if you refuse somebody.

TIP: You owe no one an explanation when you refuse to be imposed upon. You have the right to remain silent. What you don't say will not be used against you. "Sorry, I can't" is a sufficient and proper response.

If you are determined to protect the sensitivities of insensitive time-stealers, I hate to bruise your ego. But the fact is, they won't be wounded if you turn them down. They'll simply lean on someone else.

Strategy Memorize the Compassionate Refusal Process (CRP). You want to feel good about refusing someone whenever that seems to you to be the right thing to do. The process has three steps:

(1) Restate the need for the request to show you understand

(2) Give a quick, polite refusal

(3) End with your appreciation for their thinking about you

CRP reminds me of a woman we dubbed "Helen The Good" because she genuinely cared about each of her colleagues and was always going out of her way to assist anybody who asked her to do anything. Of course everybody took advantage, not suspecting that Helen was exhausted by the end of the day. After she complained to me of the strain, Helen and I practiced CRP.

What to say   Helen was confident she'd learned to use the process when she was finally able to resist George's persistence.

> **George:** "Please, Helen, I really need you to handle the statistical aspect for the panel. Please change your appointment and be with us Tuesday."
>
> **Helen:** "That's really a shame, George. I can certainly see that you need one more on the panel.(restatement) But I still can't make it on Tuesday. When I don't have a schedule conflict, I'll be glad to pinch hit. (refusal) We'll do it some other time. Thanks for asking me." (appreciation)

Use CRP if you tend to go overboard in complying because you care so much about your colleagues. They'll still love you.

When you want to refuse an office party invitation

Sometimes it's hard to say no because you're caught in an awkward situation. The office gang is planning another party, after hours. The last one got so wild that you don't want to go this time. But how can you get out of it? Easily.

> **TIP:** When the after-hours event is an official function, that's practically a command performance. Be there. It's important to your current and future positions to show team spirit and make new contacts.

Strategy   While the road to success does not depend on attending unrestrained affairs, the refusal should be simple and non-judgmental.

What To Say   When your cup of tea is their scotch on the rocks, a judicious response would be:

"I'm sorry, I won't be able to come."

On your own time, you don't have to attend any outrageous after-work event. Or, if you prefer, just stay for a few minutes and leave.

Retorts to requests masked by flattery

Having trouble speaking up for yourself may stem from your being easily conned. Maybe you just can't resist the old "you're the only one who can do it" line and consequently load yourself with more than you can handle.

> **TIP:** Just because someone asks, you don't have to accept. The caller is usually more concerned with getting the work done than with who is doing it.

Strategy   Suggest a substitute. This works because the person asking you has one main aim, to find someone (anyone) who can fill the assignment and it doesn't have to be you. It just has to be somebody who performs as well (or nearly as well) as you do.

Deena tried to get Karl to organize an office softball team. Although he enjoyed the game, Karl didn't have time to coordinate an after-hours work-related activity.

What to say   Note how Karl responded to Deena's request, helping her while at the same time turning her down.

> **Deena:**   "Karl, you are the only one who can successfully head this project."
>
> **Karl:**   "I'm flattered that you thought about me, Deena, but I really think Stan's your man."

This polite refusal not only suggested a substitute, but also let Karl return the favor for Stan's getting him on the hook so often.

Using the "no" sandwich

Do you want so badly for everybody to be your pal that it embarrasses you to refuse your office friends? If you want to say no without creating hard feelings, then master this popular technique known as the "no" sandwich.

> **TIP:** Colleagues who impose upon you are not your friends. Since a direct "no" may not be received well, it's easier to offer an excuse. Offer them a "no" sandwich which consists of two slices of compliments supporting a legitimate-excuse refusal.

Strategy

(1) Use the time while listening to the request to word your three-part response—compliment, excuse, compliment.
(2) Take a deep breath with your lips zipped instead of blurting out an acceptance.

Ina's difficulty was that she would grant a favor and then be furious at herself for being unable to decline.

What to say   Then she got the hang of the "no" sandwich.

> **Gayle:**   "Ina, we'll be developing a plan for employee incentives. I know that interests you. Come on, you can squeeze in one more meeting."
>
> **Ina:**   "That's thoughtful of you (beginning compliment) to remember my interest in incentives, Gayle. Unfortunately, I can't come because all my spare time is spent preparing four proposals for next month (excuse filling). One of these days I'll have the pleasure of working with you again."(ending compliment)

You'll be pleased with yourself when you can graciously say "thanks, but no thanks" while making the other person feel good about being turned down.

A pep talk to overcome indecision

Do you agonize over every decision? Do you stare ten minutes at a luncheon menu, weighing the merits of corn over beans when it's all a bunch of succotash?

If you vacillate over minor matters, speechless lest you make a mistake, let me remind you that there's no such thing as a perfect decision. Making mistakes is inevitable. Everybody does. Your objective is to free yourself to speak up.

> **TIP:** When you are wishy-washy about a decision, it affects other people's work as well as yours. The key is to take action. Don't let the operation get bogged because you have to be begged.

Strategy   Find ways to talk yourself out of the state of indecision. This four-part method should fortify your self-confidence.

(1) Quickly gather the information. Use the phone to track down any missing data.

(2) Imagine the worst possible outcome that might happen as a result of your decision. If you can face that, you can face anything.

(3) Resist shuffling papers from pile A to pile C and decide. Get the decision off your desk or call in your answer, because for minor matters it's not going to make much difference to anyone either way your decide.

(4) Map out a plan of action for major decisions. Before you begin an assignment, be clear on your goals, objectives, milestones and time frames. Each new choice grows out of ones you've already made. You simply align your new decisions with the carefully thought-out plan.

Jo-Jo is immobilized by the fear of making wrong choices. For instance, when her team was assigned to develop a plan for integrating three separate divisions into one unified operation, each team member was responsible for a given segment. After careful study, Jo-Jo prepared her part, addressing the stated goals. Then she started picking it apart, doubting her good judgment and knowledge and delaying past the deadline.

What to say   Jo-Jo knows her indecisiveness will hold her back, so we worked out a countermeasure, a pep talk to give herself.

> ***Jo-Jo:***   "Should I turn this in or make more calls for back-up data? Should I check with some others first? Should I...?"

Inner Voice: "If this isn't what the boss had in mind, he's not going to fire you over it. The worst is that you'll have to do it over, but that's better than being paralyzed. Besides, you know the operation so well that most of your decisions have to be good ones. Stop stalling and decide."

Jo-Jo got good results with this pep talk. Try it if your confidence needs bolstering before you feel free to talk or act.

When and How to Interrupt an Interruption

Some workers, although aware that they fall behind when they're unnecessarily interrupted, still say nothing. They're embarrassed to stop their peers from imposing on their time or they don't know how to excuse themselves gracefully.

How to muzzle gabbers

The common open-office layout, with no doors invites interruptions. So it's especially important to cut unwanted conversations short without offending the people you'll have to keep working with everyday.

TIP: To complete a rush assignment, turn your chair around so that people passing by can't catch your eye to interrupt you. If possible, tell the switchboard to hold your calls for two hours while you're in a meeting (with yourself). You might even hang a "Don't Disturb—Thinker At Work" sign near your desk.

Strategy Send the interrupter strong, unmistakable signals. Stand up and walk to the door or the end of your space. Politely but firmly say you can't talk now.

Maisie arrived an hour early for work, intent on making a dent in her stack of reports before the team trickled in and the phone sounded off. Riley also got to the office early. And he plopped down in the chair by her desk, sipping his coffee, and bantering. In less than 30 seconds, Maisie figured this conversation was not helping her.

What to say   Maisie got up from her chair and escorted Riley out the door after this exchange.

> **Riley:**   "Did I tell you the joke about the boss who. . ."
>
> **Maisie:**   "Riley, I'd love to chat, but you'll have to excuse me now. I have a tight deadline to meet."

Those people who come in early to relax and get warmed up have to find each other. They are perfectly happy to let you work while they seek someone else who does want to talk.

Cutting prolonged phone calls short

Are your time estimates for various tasks frequently off the mark because you spend too much time on the phone? Are you concerned that you're behind schedule, but don't want to sound curt or abrupt by hanging up?

> **TIP:**   Use an egg-timer to practice collecting all the information you need from talkative co-workers. This not only forces you to keep to the issue, but can be fun as you try to beat-the-clock. You win each time you can scramble (or unscramble) all the facts you need in three minutes.

Strategy   Utter a polite sign-off immediately after concluding your business.

What to say   Try some variation of these "hang up" lines.

> "I've taken up too much of your time. Thanks again."
>
> "Let's hold that for when we have lunch on Friday."
>
> "I'd like to talk longer, but I'm due at a meeting in two minutes. See you soon."

Get that receiver down a second after your "goodbye," before they start talking again.

Hang up—don't hang on

Quickly and gently returning the telephone receiver to its cradle is an office survival skill you must master. You are as busy as your colleagues and your time is just as important. Speak up before they can put you on hold.

TIP: Be in control of your time instead of being enslaved by a receiver. When you absolutely have to hold, keep near the phone a stack of unanswered mail or reading to be scanned. Or do isometrics or clean out your desk drawer.

Strategy Be fast with your response so that you won't be left dangling.

Roy needed to verify some dates that were in a letter sent to Jason. During previous calls, Roy found Jason's secretary accommodating, but busy. She frequently put him on hold before he could say anything else. If he did get through to Jason, he was again kept holding.

What to say Politely interrupt while the other person is still on the line.

> **Jason's Secretary:** "Jason is on the other line. Please ho–."
>
> **Roy:** "Please ask Jason to call me back just as soon as he gets off the phone." (Click)
>
> **Jason:** "I know the letter you want. Hold on while I have my secretary retrieve–"
>
> **Roy:** "Jason, please call me back just as soon as you can find it. Thanks." (Click)

It's a real time-saver to speak up and hang up instead of hanging on.

An exit line for coffee klatschers

Sometimes interruptions are worth the time. A quick walk to the water cooler can recharge your batteries, especially if you bump into a colleague and exchange useful information. The problem comes when a daily ten-minute coffee break gradually stretches to a daily half-hour and by the end of the week you're tense trying to catch up.

> **TIP:** Take a break when you need it, but remember why you're at work. You can leave the group without appearing critical of them. Just talk about your deadline.

Strategy Deliver a smiling, friendly exit line that puts the emphasis on yourself.

What to say Keep it simple.

- "I have to get back for a meeting."
- "I'm so far behind, it'll be Christmas before I catch up."

When you talk about yourself, you won't sound as if you're passing judgment on your peers. Perhaps your example will help them wise up as well, but that's not your problem.

How to Ask for Help Without Looking Helpless

Maybe it's too hard for you to ask for assistance. Perhaps you're too shy to speak up or afraid you'll look foolish, ignorant, or incapable. You must realize that the next person isn't even thinking about you. He's too busy worrying about himself.

Getting assistance when you're new

Ask your colleagues to help you. No matter how well experienced you are, if you're the new kid on the block, you are not expected to know how things are done at the new site. You need all the pieces to work the puzzle and keep from making serious mistakes. Despite the instructions given you, you probably have a ton of questions and you can't keep running back to your boss. Remember, your objective is to pass your probationary period.

> **TIP:** It's not considered a sin, but a sign of strength, to ask for guidance. Your colleagues understand that you need help because at one time they, too, were new and apprehensive. If you put everyone together who's scared stiff before taking on a new assignment, you'd have a human petrified forest.

Strategy Ask your peers for advice. Everyone loves to give it. Don't you? Actually, you are paying a compliment when you ask for this kind of assistance. You are saying, in effect, they know more than you do and you value their thinking.

What to say Try:

> "I'd really appreciate your advice on processing this data…"

Ask questions. Without help, you'll never make it to the top. You'll only make it out the door.

How to accept help when it's offered

A martyr act fools no one but the martyrs. They make it extremely obvious that they are burdened with work for the cause of the company in an attempt to call more attention to themselves.

TIP: Accept the help you need. Be a team player, not a loner. If you turn down help from your peers, it can cause resentment and rumors.

Strategy Be gracious. Even though you are terribly efficient, occasionally allow others, who are just trying to be friendly, to work with you.

Eadie is an administrative assistant who takes care of a million details by herself. She neither asks for nor accepts help, but complains that she has to do everything because no one else will. The truth is, she enjoys having the whole office dependent upon her.

But Eadie was hurt. She felt she was being ostracized. Why am I being shunned, she asked, when I try so hard and give so much of myself to the organization?

What to say Eadie was shocked to learn how her peers perceived her. However, it was easy enough to turn the perception around. She started being a team player by offering to help and by responding to any offers in a friendly, warmhearted manner.

> ***Lorna:*** "Eadie, let me give you a hand with those tabulations."

> *Eadie:*   "Thanks, Lorna, I appreciate all the help I can get."

Eadie's life was a lot easier once she was willing to change the script.

Obtaining support when your promotion is stalled

You can be too good for your own good. So good that your boss thinks you have to stay where you are because you can't be replaced. If you know you're qualified for a promotion, but you've made yourself indispensable in your present position, there are ways to win the support you need.

> **TIP:**   Look around, your salvation may be sitting at the next desk. Teach someone else your job; your moving up the organization could hinge on it.

Strategy   Your goal is to be promoted. Prove to the boss that your current work would continue to proceed smoothly if you were to advance. To accomplish this, train others in your specialty to take your place.

Kim was in a frustrating position. Her work was universally acknowledged as fantastic and her boss thought she was indispensable. Although she received good salary raises, she was stuck at the same level. And Kim wanted a promotion. I suggested that she choose two potential successors, asking them to join in a mutually beneficial plan. It would help Kim who wanted to move up, the peers who'd be learning a new skill, and their boss who wanted uninterrupted good performance.

What to say   Kim explained her situation to Andrea and Pete and found them surprisingly receptive.

> *Kim:*   "Until this is authorized, would you be willing to work during lunch hour to learn to administer the tests?"
>
> *Andrea:*   "Yes, I'd love to. That fascinates me."
>
> *Pete:*   "I've been anxious to pick up some new skills. Thanks for the chance."

Whenever Kim submitted her progress reports, she included the training project. Once assured that Andrea and Pete were doing well, the boss authorized regular working hours for continued training. Andrea and Pete became so proficient that Kim was able to enjoy a vacation and two months later her promotion came through. But nothing would have changed if Kim hadn't been willing to ask her colleagues for help.

* * *

If you want to make progress, speak up and speak out. Otherwise, you are drifting around in circles. It's okay to cause an occasional ripple because a ripple isn't a tidal wave. You won't go under for the third time when you open your mouth. On the contrary, you will be allowing your conversation to keep you on the course you have plotted for yourself.

CHAPTER 8

$$\overline{}$$

Four Guidelines for Criticizing Your Peers

QUIZ #8. HOW SKILLFULLY DO YOU CRITICIZE YOUR PEERS?

What's your criticizing quotient (CQ)? Each yes answer to the following questions is worth ten percent. To increase your skill, work on the ones under your no answers.

	YES	NO
1. Do I leave my adversaries their self respect by getting the knot out of problems instead of rapping them?	( )	( )
2. Do I calmly voice my annoyance instead of bottling it up or exploding?	( )	( )
3. Will I claim the blame for the whole group in order to get questions out in the open so we act, not react?	( )	( )
4. Do I cushion and couple my criticism with offers of help?	( )	( )
5. Will I let the appointed authority settle a colleague's nonperformance rather than lacing into the shirker myself?	( )	( )
6. Instead of backing my opponents into a corner to prove them wrong, do I tact-		

fully soften the sting and let them save
their self esteem?   ( )   ( )

7. When my colleagues are having a problem, will I spare them my lectures and
either lend a hand or shut my mouth?   ( )   ( )

8. Do I offer my idea while something can
still be done about it rather than criticize like a Monday morning quarter-
back?   ( )   ( )

9. Do I spell out the specific charge rather
than stop with critical generaliza-
tions?   ( )   ( )

10. Do I keep quiet about a colleague's past
mistake rather than keep retrying the
person for the same crime?   ( )   ( )

HOW TO VOICE DISAPPROVAL TO IMPROVE THE SITUATION

Minding your manners is easy as long as everyone else does too. However, if an argument ensues, good breeding often unravels, shedding with it the desired result.

Some talented few have sharpened their wit to the point where they can utter a clever, humorous remark to soften criticism. Take, for example, Winston Churchill's classic description of Clement Attlee: "A modest little man with much to be modest about." But most of us don't have this talent. When we zing our colleagues, the arrows often boomerang. And people who "give it to you straight" reveal their own bias.

Nevertheless, there is an effective way to deliver criticism and bring about positive changes. If you'll let your colleagues keep their pride in tact, you can verbally whack them around and they'll take it in good spirits. These four guidelines for giving criticism are a reminder to be kinder:

- Blame the method, not the motive
- Level specific charges
- Speak gently—let them keep their dignity
- Propose assistance and skip the divine guidance

Blame the Method, Not the Motive

Successful fault finding begins with self control. The temptation is great to *presume* to know why somebody else did something we don't like. ("He's only doing that to get revenge." "She's trying to make herself look more important than the rest of us.") That diagnosis starts us on the wrong track. We dig the scalpel into the person instead of the problem.

To make effective changes with the least offense, stick to the impersonal issue. Criticize the operation, the procedure, the rule, the plan. Search for new options or alternatives to your existing method.

What to say to a peer who is undermining you

You suspect a few colleagues are playing dirty tricks, interfering with your work for their own advantage. Of course you're exasperated. Your first reaction is to unload both barrels in a confrontation.

TIP: If you let your anger explode, the sweet taste of revenge evaporates quickly and you still won't have resolved the conflict. Your objective is an improved system over the current set up that caused the problem in the first place.

Strategy

(1) Reduce the tension with your opponent.

(2) Ask your peers to join you in finding ways to tighten or change the current system or method.

Meg thought she was being undermined. She was almost positive that, because of jealousy, Julian had been sabotaging some work to make himself look good. She said he was as trustworthy as a rattlesnake, slithering around the front desk intercepting or delaying important phone messages. But Meg could only guess Julian's motives. And rather than crawl on his level, I suggested she become the snake charmer and try to change the irritating condition.

What to say

(1) Instead of skinning Julian's hide, Meg would extract any venom from her own vocabulary.

(2) She'd approach Julian with established phrases that would let the two of them disagree more pleasantly: "It seems to me that," "Perhaps the question is," "You may be right, but," "That may be so, however consider that..."

(3) She'd move to get a more efficient message system by seeking peer support:

Meg: "I know you've all been upset that some important phone messages are delayed or lost. You know, gang, we need to develop a better system for receiving messages. What do you think we should do?"

By concentrating on method (getting a better message system) instead of motive (Julian will do anything to get ahead), Meg was able to reduce Julian's interference. He may still be a snake, but that's his worry.

What to say when your cohort fouls up

Sometimes a colleague fails to act responsibly and it upsets the whole office. Again, you're tempted to rip into the offender. Again, there's a better way. Your aim is to improve the system or procedures.

TIP: Let a mole hill remain a mole hill. Step up and claim the blame as though you and every other team member were responsible. "*We* have a problem..."

Strategy

(1) Get the issue out in the open where it can be discussed objectively.

(2) Let the appointed authority deal with a subordinate's goof up or poor attitude—that's a manager's job.

Because Sidney neglected his responsibility to inform Cynthia, the new administrator, about the priority policy for getting material typed, she inadvertently got everything off schedule. Cynthia started to tear Sidney apart when Dennis, a seasoned manager, showed his leadership.

What to say　Note how Dennis moved the criticism away from the offender by asking the whole group to share in recommending changes in the method.

> **Cynthia:**　"If Sidney hadn't been so sloppy, we wouldn't have this..."
>
> **Dennis:**　"Obviously, we have a problem. Now what should be done about it? Should we suggest another procedure for the manual? Better communication? Taping rules to the typing tray? Let's give our ideas to the boss, along with a brief background, to get this settled."

Sidney was so glad he escaped a serious reprimand that he resolved to get his act together. The boss posted new rules and everyone went back to work. It pays to claim the blame when you can change the procedures.

How to untangle problems without unravelling people

You're responsible for a project and one of your peers won't follow through. Keep in mind that nobody likes criticism. If you let discussions degenerate into acrimonious attacks, you'll end up looking bad. Trying to make things as hot as possible for your adversary is playing with fire and you'll probably get singed by the flames. Your objective is to settle your difficulties in a civil manner and move on.

> **TIP:**　Cushion and couple your criticism with offers of help. Let the appointing authority settle the matter when peers won't cooperate.

Strategy　Censor yourself. Don't say anything you don't want repeated because, most assuredly, it will be. If you habitually utter comments that range from snapping and sniping to vicious and malicious, few will cry when you leave the company. Watch your telephone accusations as well as face-to-face confrontations.

Barbara, in charge of the program for the Employees Banquet, had warned Lucy, the prize chairman who had a history of dropping the ball, to produce or resign.

> ***Barbara:*** "Listen, Lucy, we need ten prizes for the banquet. Don't louse us up the way you usually do or you'll be sorry."
>
> ***Lucy:*** "Hold on, birdbrain, I know what I'm doing and I don't need any advice from you."

Lucy arrived at the event late, with only two tiny prizes.

The day after the party, the two were lacing their boxing gloves for round two. Barbara told me she was still fuming at Lucy's blunder. I asked her to focus on what was really happening. Admittedly, prize chairman Lucy was no prize package, but Barbara won the booby prize.

While it was too late this time to cushion and couple her criticism, Barbara had to restore her professional demeanor. First, she had to stop rapping Lucy and get the knot out of the problem.

What to say   When Lucy wouldn't cooperate, instead of attacking her, Barbara should have gone to their boss who had authority to resolve the problem. Now, after the event, Barbara could still recoup some lost ground by pinpointing the trouble and offering a remedy during her banquet report.

> ***Barbara:*** "Boss, I had responsibility without authority and, as you know, that doesn't work too well. For next year, I suggest that (1)...(2)...(3)..."

"You should have" is only valuable if it gives a guideline for next time. When you can't change what happened in the past, suggest how to change the method for the future.

Level Specific Charges

Until you're willing to deal with the real problem, nothing will begin to get better. Beating around the bush with bitter, caustic generalizations just stirs up a lot of turmoil. Others feel your fury, but unless you break down your charges into specific issues and spell out what ought to be, no one can get to the root cause or the solution.

When co-workers criticize you behind your back

There are infinite reasons why colleagues backbite. They may be jealous. Sometimes they feel you're condescending toward them. Or you're too pushy. Or they are afraid that your working double-time shows them up. But, whatever their worry, why allow others to continue doing what they're doing unaware that you're stewing? Your objective is to clear the air and stop the back-biting.

TIP: For certain situations, one way to reduce back-biting is to keep your ambitious plans to yourself and share safer subjects like your secret for potting petunias. Your peers won't feel as threatened.

Strategy Confront your critic with what you've heard. You can discuss and settle legitimate criticism or they can deny they meant to be critical. Make them spell out any accusations.

Bill said he'd heard from four colleagues that Amelia was criticizing him behind his back. At first he found it hard to believe because she is always so friendly to him face-to-face. This called for an immediate showdown.

What to say Bill walked over to Amelia's office to confront her.

> **Amelia:** "Hi, Bill, why the long face?"
>
> **Bill:** "Amelia, what seems to be the problem? I understand from our cohorts that you're not satisfied with something I'm working on."
>
> **Amelia:** "Why, Bill, I can't imagine what you've heard."
>
> **Bill:** "Well, Amelia, I'm sure glad you're not dissatisfied and we could get this resolved. Now I won't have to listen to those nasty rumors any more."

Amelia denied she'd been finding fault with Bill. This may or may not be true, but if she had been back-biting, Bill's confronting her put a stop to it.

Correcting actions, not criticizing attitudes

If you hope to change a colleague's belief or attitude, that's an unrealistic aim unless you possess professional counseling skills. Your goals should be do-able, so shift to what you *can* change.

TIP: Revise the specific work habit or type of job performance that's giving you a headache. Work together with your
vexing colleague on the revision.

Strategy: Since you can't erase people who rub you the wrong
way, express your criticism in a manner that can change how they
act. The objective is *to alter a clearly defined action* that affects
your work.

Alex learned this lesson soon after he lit into Bart:

> **Alex:**   "Bart, you don't care about anybody else. You are a
> selfish, self centered prima donna. You never pull
> your part of the load."
>
> **Bart:**   "I do as much as anyone else around here."

Alex hadn't minced any words. But ever since that outburst,
nothing's changed. How could it change? Alex attacked Bart's attitude, not his actions. If Bart has a personality flaw, he has to
work on that by himself.

What to say   If Alex wanted Bart to do more, he had to get the
issue out in the open where they could both act rather than react,
and come up with a more workable plan. The talk had to focus on
something they could both tackle.

> **Alex:**   "Bart, we're going to have to decide a better task dis-
> tribution. I think I'm being overworked because you
> come in late and leave early."
>
> **Bart:**   "I leave early because I work quickly and finish fast."
>
> **Alex:**   "Okay, let's re-examine the workload..."

During the discussion, Bart revealed a couple of shortcuts he
used to get done faster. Alex's resentment of Bart's attitude sub-
sided as his admiration of Bart's skills increased. Criticizing an
intangible (an attitude) gets you nowhere. Correcting the tangible
(a work assignment) does.

How to dispel an undercurrent of tension

Some colleagues give you a one-word response with a glare
that says, "You infuriate me" and never explain why they're

upset. Your aim is to get the problems resolved as soon as possible.

TIP: Verbalize your difficulty. The target of one's wrath has the right to have an issue promptly settled. A stoney stare is a childish way to criticize or convey contempt. Since the target isn't clairvoyant, all that's conveyed is confusion.

Strategy Confront the glarer and suggest a solution. Calm the waters by negotiating new procedures to deal with any specific charges. But first

(1) Simmer down and get the facts.

(2) Use the facts to interrogate.

Trudy avoided any verbal skirmishes. She was steamed at Michael but instead of telling him why, she used icy stares. All she changed was her blood pressure which climbed to the boiling point as she bottled up her anger.

What to say Michael finally asked her what was wrong.

> *Michael:* "Trudy, you're obviously upset. What's the problem? Have I offended you?"
>
> *Trudy:* "Michael, I thought when we divided the files that you'd be taking care of the Davis account. He called this morning complaining of neglect. Here's his folder. What's happening?"
>
> *Michael:* "Gee, I'm sorry. I thought you told me you wanted to hold on to Davis until he signed the contract."
>
> *Trudy:* "No, but more important, how can we make sure this doesn't happen again?"

Whether you are the glare-er or the glare-ee, it is unproductive to work with negative vibes. A few minutes discussion can clear the air. But however long it takes, reduce the tension by bringing the buried issue to the surface where it can be resolved.

Speak Gently—Let Others Keep Their Dignity

If you deliberately destroy another's ego, puncture his pride, or damage his dignity, the other person may never forgive you.

You really don't win the argument when you rob your adversaries of their self respect. They eventually get back at you, probably when you least expect it and are most vulnerable. Why acquire a life-long foe? With a little thought, you can correct the problem and allow your colleague to salvage some self respect.

Correcting colleagues without saying they're wrong

You may feel you're in an impossible situation when you can't proceed because a colleague won't admit the error and you can't complain to your mutual boss without appearing to be a pouter who lost an argument. Nevertheless, saying "you're wrong" to colleagues widens the problem by putting their pride on the line.

> **TIP:** Let your colleagues redeem their self-esteem. Your objective is to move out of the stall and go forward. The skill is to deftly reverse your direction.

Strategy Giving credit for motive (if not for method) will allow your opponent to save face. First show your willingness to listen to your opponent. Then offer a compliment ("I know you want to be fair about this") that says you know your adversary is well-intentioned. He's backed himself into a corner—give him a way out.

Sally is being stubborn. Sally is wrong, but she won't budge. Charles is stuck because he has to work with Sally who is fifteen years his senior. Although she sees his potential, she considers him an irreverent upstart. She won't give him the satisfaction of moving from her position.

What to say Charles has to give Sally a graceful way to change her mind and still save her pride.

> **Sally:** "I've double-checked the figures. These are the ones that were sent to us. This is the only way to interpret them."
>
> **Charles:** "Sally, I've always respected your work and I know how you pride yourself on accuracy. So I think you'd want to know they gave you the wrong infor-

mation. It's not your fault, so please call and give them a chance to correct the figures they sent you."

Once they agreed on the correct data, Charles went a step further with a "Let's starts over, I may be wrong" approach. Once you stop saying "You're wrong" most matters can be resolved. Your opponents already know they are wrong and are desperately seeking a face-saving retreat—which you can provide.

Being up front with your peers

Some people think that if they step on another's toes, they will somehow seem taller. Actually, such an attitude just shortens their self respect as they sink lower into the muck.

TIP: Play fair with your colleagues and hope that they, in turn, play fair with you. If they don't, you can set in motion the wheels of retribution without lifting a finger.

Strategy If you find you've been snookered, use the office grapevine to leak the story about the culprit's deceit.

Harry, trying to get a raise, developed an idea he thought would impress the boss and asked Adam to critique it. Adam assured Harry it was a fine piece of work, but later gave the boss arguments against it that he neglected to tell poor Harry. Adam cut the rug out from under him.

What Harry Said Harry nonchalantly mentioned the incident to his assistant. With typical office wall-to-wall gossip, the boss eventually learned about the duplicity and Adam got called on the carpet.

Forget a frontal attack if you're the victim of hanky-panky. The office force will be with you.

How to take the sting out of your criticism

At times it's necessary to level criticism because something your colleague does inadvertently is negatively affecting your work. Your *objective* is to accomplish change while creating the least amount of resentment.

> **TIP:** Create a calm setting so that the mistake appears easier to correct. By carefully surrounding your criticism with compliments, you further the prospects for a reasonable discussion.

Strategy Soften the sting of a complaint by wrapping it in pleasant language. Find something your colleague does that you can honestly say you like or hold in esteem. State it and restate it before and after you criticize.

Tanya was having trouble concentrating because much of Fern's work was done by long-distance telephone and Fern tended to raise her voice during these conversations.

What to say Note how gently Tanya told Fern that she talked too loud.

> **Tanya:** "Fern, one of the things I admire most about you is your animation. But I'm sure you don't realize how your voice carries in this big room. Frankly, I find it difficult to do my work when you're talking on the phone. So could you please speak a little softer?"
>
> **Fern:** "Oh, I had no idea I was disturbing you."
>
> **Tanya:** "I know you didn't. Ordinarily, I enjoy the way you express yourself. Take this morning's meeting. We'd still be in there arguing if you hadn't zeroed in on the real trouble."

Fern hardly flinched because Tanya had dulled the sharp point of her stinging remark.

Offer Assistance and Skip the Divine Guidance

Some colleagues believe they have to critique every action around the office or the sun won't rise tomorrow morning. When you keep harping "if you had only done what I said," you become a prophet without portfolio. No one wants guidance given in a high-handed manner. On the other hand, everyone can use genuine, caring support.

How to help a colleague who's made a mistake

When your colleagues goof up, they are already kicking themselves. They don't need you to kick them, too. What can help them is talking about the situation to a friend.

TIP: Be a good non-judgmental listener. Give your colleagues the opportunity to talk about the incident to you. During troublesome times, be willing to be the sponge that absorbs their anger.

Strategy Give your peers time and space to allow themselves to vent their anger.

Gordon appeared upset and Jen asked if he was having problems with the project. Gordon replied that the boss had just chewed him out for being late with it. This brought a harsh reaction from Jen.

Jen: "Gordon, you should have known that was coming. You shouldn't have expected to complete the job on time without having enough materials on hand."

He should have done this, and he should have done that. No wonder Gordon stomped off in a huff. He felt bad enough after a barrage from the boss without having Jen point up his mistakes, too.

What to say Fortunately, he bumped into Cloris who immediately sensed Gordon's anguish and lent a hand.

Cloris: "I know how you feel, Gordon. That happened to me last year. Maybe it would help you to talk about it over a cup of coffee?"

Remember, there are times we all need some friendly support just to get through a bad day.

Offering assistance early on

Monday morning quarterbacks have all the answers—too late to do any good. Their style is to grumble over the way others stumble, as in "If I had been in charge, I would have. . ."

> **TIP:** If there is still time to revise the game plan, offer your criticism. Say it then, when it will count. Being still, and waiting until after the deed has failed to say, "You should've. . " only shows you have excellent hindsight and enormous insensitivity.

Keeping quiet about a peer's past mistakes

When your colleagues have erred and paid for their mistake with remorse and embarrassment, they have the right not to have it repeatedly thrown back in their faces.

> **TIP:** Let a past mistake rest. Don't punish a colleague again for the same crime.

Strategy Help your colleagues improve by concentrating on the present and future.

Janet made a really careless mistake when she got some orders mixed up a month ago. Kay hasn't stopped reminding her about it.

What to say Janet realized this was turning into a feud and she wanted to put an end to it.

Kay: "If some people paid more attention—"

Janet: "C'mon, Kay, get off my case. I can't undo what was done. Rehashing it is a waste of time. Let's settle this now before our boss has to step in and we both get known as troublemakers "

Janet's point hit home with Kay. Neither of them wanted to get the reputation of being difficult to get along with. They knew that once you get that label, it's very hard to get rid of it. It was of mutual benefit for them to bury their differences and start working together in a friendly manner.

Keep in the back of your mind that when it is necessary to criticize, you can tear into any problem without ripping people apart. If you do tear someone or something down, you have an obligation to help rebuild. Remember that the purpose of criticizing your colleagues is not to get rid of your anger, but to improve a troublesome situation.

CHAPTER 9

Persuasion Strategies to Use When You Have No Authority

QUIZ #9. HOW PERSUASIVE ARE YOU WITH YOUR PEERS?

In each of the following situations, what would you most likely say? Interpretation below.

1. You need help from some colleagues to complete an important assignment, but they're all busy with their own work. You

    (a) promise you'll be indebted forever for the help
    (b) explain how very much you need this help
    (c) link this help with achieving their wants

2. You sometimes call your colleagues by incorrect names.

    (a) Most people have the same problem—they'll forgive you
    (b) You try more concentration, imagery, and repetition
    (c) This annoys you because you know names are important

3. When one of your peers does something quite well, you

       (a) take time to call and even drop a note to his boss

       (b) think about how you, too, might do it that way

       (c) know you pale by comparison

4.   You've just finished a proposal you want to present at the staff meeting. You think the best chance of approval is to

       (a) win over the boss before your meeting presentation

       (b) review the draft with other staffers, seeking their input

       (c) keep it secret until you spring it, retaining credit and giving opponents less time to react

5.   Generally, when you want to persuade colleagues to do something, you

       (a) swallow hard and resort to flattery

       (b) try to be sincere in complimenting their ability

       (c) level about what's involved, what's needed, and why they'd want to do it

6.   When it's especially important to you to inspire trust among your colleagues, you

       (a) try to act confident, but find it difficult

       (b) overcome any self doubt by offering a do-able plan

       (c) try to impress them by mentioning your past accomplishments

7.   Although you don't have the authority to issue orders, you desperately need several peers to participate. You

       (a) ask an influential friend to intercede

       (b) explain the request as a personal favor to you

       (c) explain the request as a personal favor to them

8.   Fellow staff members are debating a controversial issue and the argument is heating up. You

       (a) keep still until you can agree with the majority

       (b) press your point to make them see why you are right

       (c) quietly summarize the few essentials and suggest a solution

9.   When others ask you to do things you don't like which are an intrinsic part of your job, you

(a) do it graciously, conveying that you're happy to help

(b) complain you always get the worst jobs then do it anyway

(c) do it as though you are doing the other person a favor

10. During face-to-face conversations with your peers, you tend

(a) to lose concentration worrying about your next response

(b) to keep eye contact observing body language and concentrating on the key thoughts

(c) to avoid eye contact staring at the floor or out the window

Interpretation

Group I: 1b, 2a, 3c, 4c, 5a, 6c, 7a, 8b, 9b, 10c
Group II: 1a, 2c, 3b, 4a, 5b, 6a, 7b, 8a, 9c, 10a
Group III: 1c, 2b, 3a, 4b, 5c, 6b, 7c, 8c, 9a, 10b

If your answers are mostly in Group I, your colleagues hardly hear you. You are focusing so much on your own needs and wants that you are not catching the clues that could help you convince them. Try harder to relax. Stop the incessant worry about how you look to others and start listening to them.

If your answers are mostly in Group II, you are sometimes convincing. You often know what might be effective, but don't follow through. For times when you become buried in your own problems, stop for a moment. Then back away, see how everyone else is affected, and let new possibilities occur to you.

If your answers are mostly in Group III, you are usually persuasive. You follow the adage, "To sell John Smith what John Smith buys, you must see John Smith through John Smith's eyes." By asking yourself first what action is of most benefit to everyone involved, you can get your way even without having the authority.

HOW TO CONVINCE YOUR COLLEAGUES
TO FOLLOW YOUR LEAD

Remember Momma's "Eat it, you need it, you're too skinny!" That didn't persuade you, it provoked you. Momma was cramming a deficiency down your throat. She should have dangled a desire. Yours, not hers.

It's no cinch to convince. Yet there are times your persuasive powers may be all you have going for you. Especially when you don't have the authority to issue an order and you need the willing cooperation of your co-workers to get the job done. It takes practice to present your subject enthusiastically and realistically, with empathy for your peers. They may not heed your need. But *their* longing—ah, that's the lure. To convince your fellow workers to help you out:

- Massage their egos and they'll feel important
- Inspire the desire to do it your way
- Ooze self confidence to be trusted
- Sharpen your listening skills

Persuasion Strategy 1:   Say Things That Make Your Peers Feel Important

Everyone wants to be noticed. Even for those who pretend indifference, the deepest cut of all is to be ignored. Remembering that flattery falls flat, take a minute to say an honest few words that will make your co-workers feel important. Pronounce their names correctly, show that your interest goes beyond their work product, and be happy for them when something goes well.

Call colleagues by their correct names

Even if you have a problem recalling names, when it's your name that's being mangled or forgotten, you're not so quick to forgive. That's because a name is the only thing we have that's exclusively our own. It distinguishes us from the pack. It makes us feel important. Your *objective* is to pay your peers the nicest compliment you can by remembering their names.

> **TIP:** Let me answer Shakespeare's question, "What's in a name?" Call Rose by any other name and she won't act as sweet. "Violet" may make her violent. So will renaming Charles "Chuck" or "Charlie" if he wants to be called Charles. Don't take liberties with someone else's name. Get the name right.

Strategy

(1) *Visualize the name in print* to jog your memory later. Ask for their business cards or write down the name.

(2) *Repeat your colleague's name* during the conversation. Introduce that person to anyone who joins you ("Dawn, have you met Bob White?")

(3) *Practice calling your colleagues by name* whenever you pass in the hall or the street.

(4) *Study books on memory improvement* and especially practice the name-association exercises.

Tony told me he pulls a blank at the company's quarterly conferences, failing to remember names of some associates he sees only occasionally even though he's in periodic phone or mail contact with them.

What to say   Because others also have trouble connecting names with faces, I suggested he offer a practical solution to the conference coordinator.

Tony:	"Betsy, it's obvious that you put in a lot of planning time to have our conferences go so smoothly." (a transparent stroke, but true)
Betsy:	"Why thank you, I'm glad someone noticed."
Tony:	"Only one thing is missing. Some of us can't remember names. We need name tags—large ones with large felt-pen printing that can be read without a magnifying glass."
Betsy:	"That's a good suggestion, Tony. I wish I'd thought of it."

If there are no name tags when you are introduced and you can't remember the name, say "I'm sorry, I didn't catch your name." If it's unusual, ask how it's spelled to help you remember it.

Express personal interest in them

There is a life after 5:00 P.M. Your colleagues resent being thought of as one-dimensional, just known for the job they do. Egos are fragile. Everyone wants to be seen as an individual person with special needs and wants who is also a part of the world outside the office.

> **TIP:** Your *objective* is to make friends and keep the friends you make. Bend a little to get your colleagues to like you and want to help you.

Strategy Add a little small talk.

(1) Ask about whatever interests them.

(2) Ask for their opinions.

Lisa's not running for office, but she'll never know when she'll need a vote of confidence from a colleague. She told me she didn't have the time to become better friends with her peers. Together we discovered little chunks of time for personal exchanges that could show she noticed them.

What to say For instance, every morning Lisa waits for the elevator among a dozen colleagues, all standing there mute as mummies. She agreed to use the waiting time to enhance her friendships.

> **Lisa:**   "Hi, Chuck, how many miles are you running now? When is the next race?"
>
> "Lee, what do you think the board will decide on the wage issue?"

The technique is to ask questions that draw out the others and get them talking about themselves, their hobbies, and their concerns.

Applaud little successes

Most of us are quick to react when someone annoys us, but fail to act when someone pleases us. Therein lies an almost untapped way to win friends. We may mean to applaud our peers, but we get busy and forget.

> **TIP:** Before it skips your mind, call a deserving colleague. Your objective is to encourage excellence among your peers or at least a very high standard of quality. The better they are, the better the organization, the better you look.

Strategy:

(1) Call or drop by their desks to acknowledge the good work of your peers.

(2) Tell their bosses how good they were.

Rebecca, one of the attorneys from the Legal Department, addressed Lisa's directors, explaining how a new ruling would affect them.

What to say   Lisa was impressed and called Rebecca to tell her.

Lisa: "Rebecca, your talk was certainly enlightening. I just wanted to tell you how much I enjoyed it."

Rebecca: "Thank you so much, Lisa, I wasn't sure how well it went over. Thanks for calling."

Your colleagues appreciate and remember the little things you say—the quick handwritten congratulatory note or the brief "Great idea you had," the considerate "I thought this might be of interest to you since you're our expert on..." Be on the lookout and you'll find many opportunities to applaud little successes.

TIP: Be alert for articles that your colleagues may get published in professional or trade journals, or in the company newsletter. Acknowledge the insight they showed in interpreting organizational goals.

Persuasion Strategy 2: Inspire the Desire to Do it Your Way

We all prefer to feel we ourselves "bought" into an idea, rather than being conned into it. Instead of trying to talk your peers into anything, let them convince themselves. Since they see right through flattery, try telling them what's in it for them, tell them the benefits of doing the job, or break down the work so that it won't appear overwhelming. Tell them exactly what's involved, why their special skill, ability, experience, or personality is important to getting the job accomplished, and why you think they'll want to do it.

Entice others to buy into your plan

Remember the yo-yo? No matter how far you sent it spinning, the yo-yo found its way back to your hand. But when you held it too tightly, it fizzled out and you had to rewind. That's what happens if you cling too possessively to your ideas, feeling paranoid that someone else might get a little glory for your proposal.

TIP: Use sincere complimentary remarks to help gain peer participation, such as "We need people of your calibre to help us put this across" or "As an astute student of marketing trends, I'm sure you can see the importance."

Strategy Get input from your colleagues. Your aim is to have your plan accepted. Usually, colleagues' contributions will improve your work product and, once they're involved, they'll have a vested interest to see your plan approved. Here are four approaches to try.

(1) Toss a raw idea into the hopper and let your colleagues help you polish it. Allow the idea to become "ours" instead of "mine" with pride of product instead of pride of authorship.

> "Which of these three designs do you think would be more effective?"

(2) Ask co-workers to do you a favor and thereby involve them in your project.

> "Laurie, may I borrow your management book? I need some statistics. From your experience, do you think the section on absenteeism accurately represents our current situation?"

(3) Allow colleagues to feel that an idea is partially theirs or that they contributed to its formation. That makes them a part of your project and interested in its progress.

> "Wayne, I expanded on an idea you came up with at lunch the other day..."

(4) Glide away from a major decision about their involvement and ask them about a minor decision

Instead of: "Will you do it?"

Try: "Is 10:00 AM better than 3:00 PM for our meeting? Your place or mine?"

Talk about your colleagues' wants

Talk about those things *your colleagues* can relate to or value or desire rather than talking about what *you* want. Describe the sizzle (what intrigues them) and they'll buy the steak (what interests you). Your *objective* is to persuade your colleagues to do something you believe is good for all of you.

TIP: Remember, one's trivia is another's treat. Snap on your antennae so that you can catch the clues to what your colleagues want. Make a mental note of casual comments that can help you.

Strategy   Concentrate on and observe your peers. Listen to what they say. Some crave challenge, more knowledge or culture. What is it that makes each one tick?

When Josh wanted Rita to head her section for the blood drive, he remembered that she had remarked to him repeatedly how she wished she could speak in public the way Lila does.

What to say   Tempt your colleagues based on your perceptions and observations.

Josh: "Rita, by chairing the sub-committee, you'll be reporting regularly to the entire group. If you'd like, I'll help you with those reports. It's a good chance to practice your public speaking on us. You'll end up in Lila's league."

Rita: "Gee, thanks, Josh, I'd really like that."

When the talk is about our own interest, we listen more attentively and are more likely to agree.

What would you say if you were the other person

Persuading begins with pretending. When you put yourself in another person's shoes and see all issues through their eyes, for the moment you "become" the other person.

TIP: Before you speak, pretend you are holding a magnet composed of the interests of your colleagues. By talking about that magnet, you attract and keep their attention. Once you can get yourself to think the way they think, the approach and the words will become evident to you.

Strategy: Ask yourself what you would think and say if you were the other person.

To improve its public relations, Yvonne's company was "adopting" elderly nursing home patients as a community project. Yvonne was having difficulty getting volunteers. She told everyone how much the patients needed help, but this approach wasn't getting results. I asked her what goes through her mind when she gets a request to volunteer. Yvonne listed several points:

- Why am I being asked to volunteer my time?
- What's the connection between my doing this and receiving personal reward or recognition?
- How would my volunteering improve my standing with the company or make my job more secure?

What to say By answering her own questions, Yvonne armed herself with new insight and was ready to talk incentives to her peers.

> ***Yvonne:*** "Clare, we need this project to improve our public image. The plan is for twenty of us to spend two hours on Tuesdays, each "adopting" one patient, with the boss running weekly bingo games. In May, we'll honor volunteers at a luncheon—framed certificates, prizes for the most service hours, notations in the personnel file, and so on. This is a chance to help yourself along with the company and the community."

We like to help others and, in the process, if we can help ourselves or feel good about ourselves, that's even more appealing.

Make it sound like fun to follow you

Occasionally you may notice things are dull around your office and your team seems to be slowing down. You want to generate a little excitement among your subordinates. One way to accomplish this is to issue a challenge to one of your peers.

TIP: Issue a challenge by proposing contests or organizing competitive teams both within your unit and among other units. Carefully think through all aspects of any contest before your start, including the rules and prizes.

Strategy Make whatever you want done sound like it would be a pleasant experience, not more pressure, even though your aim is to increase the quantity or quality of the work product. To favorably influence the results, express your own enthusiasm.

When Jessie wanted to create more team spirit within her division, she decided to hold contests. The competitive teams, she said, would sound easy and be fun for everyone.

What to say I suggested she might begin by tossing a challenge to another division director to arouse the competitive spirit among her own people.

> **Jessie:** "Bruce, I bet you a steak dinner our division will outproduce yours in the next month."
>
> **Bruce:** "You're on. No way can you beat us."

Telling her group about the bet produced an even better result than Jessie expected. Every one of her subordinates wanted to be in on the bet with the members of Bruce's division. The losers good naturedly hosted the winners when the entire group of both teams had a joint luncheon, with both sides bragging about their increased productivity. It was interesting that the respective staff members worked harder for their "team" than they had ever worked for themselves in a contest among individuals. In fact, pitting individuals against individuals could prove more divisive than productive. Your contest should inspire cooperation among co-workers and instill pride in being part of the team's success.

Persuasion Strategy 3: How to Get Them to Trust You

After you've picked up steam, people are quick to jump aboard your train. But how do you get the train rolling in the first place?

Project self-assurance you don't yet feel

What your peers believe or perceive about you is more real to them than reality. So act the part. Show self-assurance even if you don't feel it yet. The impression you give about yourself is more persuasive than anything anybody else can say.

> **TIP:** Come up with a plan, because presenting a plan inspires confidence. Your *objective* is to have your peers feel confidence in you even though you wield no power to tell them what to do.

Strategy

(1) *Sound as though what you want done is do-able.* Limit the plan to what is actually required—the exact needs and minimum effort—to make it work. Break this up into manageable chunks, asking each one to do his or her specialty so as not to burden anyone. Show honest appreciation of talent by explaining why the deed won't happen without them.

> "We've just gotten a rush assignment, Betty. I don't think we can get it out on time without your calculating speed. Could you please work up these estimates for us?"
>
> "Ordinarily, Roger, we could do it in my unit. But yours is the only one with expertise to deal with the special..."

(2) *Ask politely, but firmly.* Instead of implying that you're smarter or the only one who knows what's needed, portray a modest and inoffensive manner and refrain from commanding, telling, or apologizing. But more importantly, don't beg anyone to do you a personal favor. Point out that their participation is actually a personal favor to them.

> "Art, the boss will certainly be pleased to hear how you pitched right in when we needed you."

(3) *Explain how the company will be affected.* Indicate the projected benefits.

> "The boss says this is important. Getting this order should pull us ahead of the competition."

TIP: Once the crisis is past, assure cooperation next time by sending brief thank-you notes or calling each one who helped. Prepare memos for your boss's signature to teammates' supervisors telling the results accomplished because of their help, and send blind copies to your teammates.

Come across as poised when others lose control

You and your colleagues are debating a controversial matter and gradually tempers start to flare. Someone puts you down. It's annoying, but that's an action you can turn around to your own advantage.

TIP: Let the others rant and rave. While your peers carry on, you can carry off their respect. Keep your poise while the others are yelling at each other.

Strategy Your objective is to be seen as someone always in control, someone everybody can count on in a crisis.

The group was talking about the need to purchase some new equipment. Kurt observed that the discussion was sinking to an insulting level. In command of himself while everyone else got excited, he was able to swallow any personal digs and concentrate on reaching a good decision.

What to say Note how the contrast of Kurt's quiet self-confidence inspires confidence.

Bud: "That's a stupid idea. We need a new billing machine now if we are going to..."

Leslie: "Look who's being stupid! The priority here is..."

Kurt: "Look, folks, what we are saying really boils down to the best time to buy the new machine—now or in six months."

This kind of cool, reasonable mediation from Kurt, time after time, won him the respect and confidence of his peers.

Let them know you're a team player

You have greater influence among your colleagues when you earn their trust. Besides projecting self-assurance and always being in control of yourself, they'll trust you more when they know they can depend on you to come through day after day, as a member of the team.

TIP: Be happy to pitch in and help out. Do your job cooperatively, without quibbling or grumbling. You are going to do it anyway, why not be gracious and score some "persuasion" points in the process?

Strategy   Signal that you're glad to carry your share, and more if necessary. Your objective is to inspire confidence among your colleagues by talking as a team player.

Beth was responsible for analyzing monthly figures she received from unit leaders over whom she had no authority. Instead of getting everyone to pull together, she alienated herself from them by requiring unnecessary paperwork. Consequently, they delayed doing the reports until they could find the time and Beth was always complaining about the lack of cooperation

What to say   Beth agreed to let them know she wanted to help them by removing any stumbling blocks. She arranged a meeting with all the unit leaders.

Beth: "I realize it's been too time-consuming for you to get out the monthly reports on time. How do you think we can streamline the forms? What can I do to help you get the reports done?"

Her desire to be a team player came through loud and clear. Together, they designed a new form limited to essential data the boss needed to know. Beth, the bottleneck, became Beth, their trusted ally.

Persuasion Strategy 4:   Sharpen Your Listening Skills

When we were taught to speak, read, and write, listening skills went in one ear and out the other. We usually remember only a fraction of what we hear. Sometimes we turn a deaf ear because of a preconception, retaining only what we expected to be told. Or we sift what we can relate to and tune out the rest.

TIP: Listen carefully when a colleague's brainchild is under discussion so that you can ask pointed, penetrating questions. Although you're no expert on that topic, you will still be *perceived* as wise and well-informed.

Strategy   To become more persuasive among your peers, develop these seven listening skills:

1.   *Keep Eye Contact.* Some people come across as inattentive and ineffective because they have a habit of looking out the window, down on the floor, and staring at their hands during a one-to-one conversation. It's easy to overcome this by sitting straight, not slouched, and leaning slightly forward in your chair. By constantly looking the other person in the eye—even when the phone rings or a voice drifts in from the next room—you show definite interest. You can then focus on what the other person is really saying.

2.   *Stroke the Speaker.* Are you so worried about how you are going to answer a possible question that you also appear preoccupied? Before it's your turn to make a point, let the speaker feel your interest and know you understand with a smile, a nod, or an "I see." Repeat or paraphrase the essence of a comment you heard with "Let me see if I grasp your concept. . ."

3.   *Concentrate Without Interrupting.* Even if your colleague's idea seems impractical, consider the time that went into it. Don't jump in to argue in defense of your point until the presenter completes the thought. Listen with an open mind without letting your ego plug up your ears.

4.   *Listen for the Main Thought.* Why clutter your brain with stacks of specifics? If you're taking notes, jot down only key words

and phrases. When you try to remember everything you are hearing, you get confused attempting to recall a series of stats or a ream of reasons. ("Did he say five or ten percent after the first four years?") Whatever it was, it was a minor detail you can check out later should you need to know it.

5. *Connect What is Being Said to Your Own Interests.* When a dry subject bores you, relate it to something you are interested in. If you don't care about the yield increase from certain edible plants, link the increase to your concern for people who are starving. Doing that expends less energy than faking attention. It takes discipline, but the alternative is limiting yourself to inconsequential banter.

6. *Use the Extra Time—You Think Faster Than the Speaker Speaks.* Thought is quicker than speech. While the other person is getting the words out, you have extra time to anticipate what the speaker will say next. In your head, summarize what's been said. Decide how well the speaker is supporting his or her position and whether or not you agree.

7. *Tune in to What isn't Said.* You can't reach people unless you catch what they are—and are not—saying. Observe others carefully:

- Do facial expressions and gestures match the words?
- Are they saying "yes" while gritting their teeth with a plastic smile or gesturing with a shrug?
- Do they claim to be excited about an idea but talk in a slower, lowered voice, at a stiff and controlled pace?
- Why do they remain silent?
- Is there an implied meaning to the comment "You'll never know how much this means to me"?
- Ask yourself questions: "Why did he look away when I mentioned renewing the order?" "Did she just stifle a yawn? Does this subject bore her?" "Are his remarks just a little too glib? Does he seem a little too attentive?"

Tricia kept missing signals others were sending because instead of concentrating on their words, she was deciding on her next comment. She learned to use the time differential for listening and evaluating. For example, she "heard" that Mark wasn't as all-fire sure about the plan as she had supposed and therefore altered her reply from going along with it to pointing out a couple of problems.

> **Mark:** "Sometimes I wonder if we're doing the right thing, Tricia, but then I consider that the project's been approved and it's full steam ahead."
>
> **Tricia:** "It seems to me that the plan is solid except for two things..."

* * *

Much of your persuasive success depends on your ability to listen and observe. Once you can detect what your colleague wants, search for some way to link that desire with whatever it is you want done. Persuading your peers to follow your lead is a legitimate activity when everyone benefits from it.

CHAPTER 10

How to Capture the Attention of Your Peers

QUIZ #10. DO YOU HAVE YOUR PEERS' ATTENTION?

On a scale of 1 to 5, with 1 being seldom and 5 usually, how often do you exhibit these conversational and group discussion skills?

		1	2	3	4	5
1.	You try to be brief and come directly to the point by trimming the trivia.	( )	( )	( )	( )	( )
2.	You read enough to keep current and store interesting items to contribute.	( )	( )	( )	( )	( )
3.	You steer conversations to topics beyond your interest to that of your listeners.	( )	( )	( )	( )	( )
4.	Whenever possible, you add interest and color with examples and analogies.	( )	( )	( )	( )	( )
5.	When the discussion gets muddled, you ask questions that bring the issue into focus.	( )	( )	( )	( )	( )

6. You avoid prefacing your comments with an apology.   ( )( )( )( )( )

7. You practice saying precisely what you mean, studying subtle nuances.   ( )( )( )( )( )

8. You spot an opening and jump in, not one to be silent the whole time.   ( )( )( )( )( )

9. You can be spirited and forceful without being opinionated and unpleasant.   ( )( )( )( )( )

10. You control your annoyance by starting with a point of agreement or an opponent's admirable quality.   ( )( )( )( )( )

11. You practice yielding, giving the other person equal time.   ( )( )( )( )( )

12. You're always yourself, not an imitation of someone else.   ( )( )( )( )( )

13. You poke fun at unquestioned routines or exaggerate to make a point.   ( )( )( )( )( )

14. You vary your volume and inflection to prevent a monotone.   ( )( )( )( )( )

15. You prepare your staff meeting reports and resist racing through the delivery.   ( )( )( )( )( )

16. You bolster your confidence and increase effectiveness with cryptic reminder notes.   ( )( )( )( )( )

17. When reporting you wait for quiet instead of outshouting the noisy or rude.   ( )( )( )( )( )

18. You utilize visuals and other programming techniques to help clarify a report.   ( )( )( )( )( )

19. You arrange questions or points in logical order before you dial the phone.   ( )( )( )( )( )

20. After placing a call, you immediately identify yourself.   ( )( )( )( )( )

21. You say you'll call back rather than faking an answer or heming or hawing.   ( )( )( )( )( )

22. You answer each call as if it might be from the president of your company.   ( )( )( )( )( )

23. You avoid saying anything face-to-face or on the phone that you don't want repeated.   ( )( )( )( )( )

HOW TO SNAG ATTENTION WHEN SPEAKING TO COLLEAGUES

Are you so afraid of making a fool of yourself that if they gave you the floor you'd want to go through it? Would you rather walk on nails than stand and speak before the people you work with every day?

In Chapter 3, we discussed conquering the panic of prepared presentations before your boss or top management. Now let's surmount the obstacles when verbal communication with your peers deprives you of their respect and makes you feel inadequate, uncomfortable, or even ill. It may happen during face-to-face and telephone conversations or committee and staff meeting discussions and reports.

The way to gain self-confidence is to build from a solid base. Concentrate on:

- Adding zest and consideration to conversations
- Snagging attention at meetings—being prepared, practiced, and pleasant

- Improving your telephone techniques
- Coming across as impressive—incisive and decisive

Four Techniques to Capture Attention in Conversations

Even though you know you are capable of good contributions, do you feel you're a fiasco when speaking with your peers? Do you hear your response in your head, unable to open your mouth? Or do you know you're dragging out your comments? Do you feel compelled to preface each remark? Do you resent those always on top of the latest news?

You can overcome these common conversational faults. Focus your attention on and practice the following conversational techniques.

1. Get right to the point

Maybe you have plenty of great ideas, but nobody's listening if, before you can get them across, someone shouts, "What are you trying to say?" Bear in mind that your ideas have to compete with a barrage of thoughts encircling everyone. What you say has to be sharp enough to penetrate the protective barrier each of us puts up in order to handle the onslaught of thoughts.

TIP: Be brief or you're a bore. Tell your story quickly, hitting the high spots and trimming the trivia.

Strategy Get to the point by sharpening a pencil.

(1) Draw diagrams. Picture a scale of pros and cons to visualize which facts have more weight.

(2) Jot down your point, limiting your words. Wait to relate it, even indirectly, to something somebody has just said.

Gina is a bright researcher whose desire to be thorough made her come across as wordy. She was meek and miserable during conversations with colleagues. They teased her so much with "Get to the point" that she hesitated to join in. I suggested to Gina that she apply one of her research skills to talking—the ability to isolate a point and relate it to other points.

What to say Tie your remark to a previous one. Relate it to something the listener is interested in and can identify with.

Nelson: "The project has no impetus, nothing to get it moving."

Gina: "I have an idea that could help you get the extra momentum you mentioned. What if we added a new section for...?"

Gina now makes the point quickly and briefly because she learned to summarize her thoughts before opening her mouth.

TIP: Practice plotting ahead. Think it through. "If they say (this)..., then I'll say (that)..." If someone interrupts you while you're making your point, hold your own and continue confidently with your contribution:

> "Yes, that's (true) (important) (may be so), but first I'd like to tell you that..."

---

2. *Grab immediate attention*

You don't need practice swings before you bat. No one's interested in your apologies. The aim is to present your point with poise and confidence.

TIP: Start with a punch that gets them listening to you. An apology turns everyone off. Consider it a cardinal sin to express real or pretended modesty before you give an opinion.

Strategy Begin in a positive way.

(1) Grit your teeth to avoid any preface which destroys the power of the comment, such as

> "Forgive my ignorance, but..." "I really don't know anything about the subject, yet it seems to me that..." "I'm sorry I didn't have time to..."

(2) Jump right in with the point you want to make, eliminating the poorly worded warm-up.

What to say   Why pretend ignorance and be regarded as a conceited phony when you are about to speak wisely and can be regarded as a leader?

> "We could really make gigantic leaps if we were to..."
> "What about beating them at their own game? I propose that we..."

3. Store up engrossing items to relate or compare

For the battle with the brain, unlike the battle with the bulge, you have to indulge. Do enough reading, listening, and studying so that you can offer contributions to the conversations. If you limit yourself to small talk, eventually all you can dig into is the freshest dirt.

TIP: Your objective is to monopolize attention for a few minutes. The newspaper can serve as a drill book if you'll make notes of an occurrence that interests you and then try out your ideas about it on a friend.

Strategy
(1) Keep up with what's happening both generally and in your field.
(2) Know one subject thoroughly.
(3) Talk in technicolor.

What to say

(1) Summarize, then give your own interpretation about what's been reported. After you repeat the meat of a print, radio, or TV editorial, say for example:

> "I think we're going to feel the effects of that Supreme Court ruling locally when..."

(2) Be it modern jazz or ancient Greeks, becoming an authority on any subject that fascinates you helps you hold your head up and appear more forceful. Let's say your hobby is birdwatching, you can find ways to work this knowledge into the conversation and give it some life.

"That shade of scarlet is exquisite. Reminds me of the red-winged blackbird."

(3)   Enrich the picture with examples and analogies.

Bland: "The people were very poor."

Colorful: "If the Jones's had meat more than once a week they knew it was a national holiday."

4. Ask questions that zero in on the issues

Asking a question that brings the problem back into focus makes you even more important to the discussion than the person who answers you.

TIP: Once you survive a question, next time try prefacing the query with a comment. If you wonder why they do things in such a complicated way, maybe because that was never questioned. A polite, careful inquiry can win you favorable notice: "I wonder, would it be possible to. . .?"

Strategy   Your *objective* is to detect the salient point, the one that stands out from the rest. Strip away the non-essentials and get down to the core. Ask yourself what you really need to know.

There was Megan sitting in a crowded room. She thought she was the only one confused by the new procedure Jeff just proposed. I had suggested when she found herself in such situations that she look around at the faces. She stole a glance at Gregory. The others looked similarly puzzled.

What to say   At times like these, act quickly. Grab the chance.

Megan: "How much time and money would be saved by having messengers pick up paychecks at the central office and distribute them at the worksites?"

Jeff: "Glad you brought that up. We figure. . ."

When you ask incisive questions that cut through the verbage, people will pay attention when you speak.

Five Techniques to Capture Attention at Meetings

No matter how hard you try, if there is any way for people to misinterpret what you say, they will find it. So aim to express yourself with control, accuracy, and clarity. These five techniques will help you.

1. Participate in smaller groups as preparation

Whenever you want to give your opinion at meetings, do your lips freeze? Are you so petrified that you'll sound ridiculous to the group that you sit there speechless? Well, get up off the rack. The torture is self-imposed and the situation can be self-corrected.

TIP: The *objective* is to bolster your confidence so that you'll feel free to participate. Come to your meetings prepared with notes, pen, and pad. Write large enough to read your writing with a quick downward glance. With this excellent reference, you won't fumble for the right word, name, or statistic. Your notes will restrain you from rambling, and your sharpness will generate support for your suggestion.

Strategy

   (1) Write yourself a script before you get the stage.
   (2) Get additional practice by speaking at very small committee meetings.

Jennifer was wallowing in pity because she had good ideas but nothing came out at the meeting. She couldn't open her mouth. I urged her to join some committee that interested her. The smaller, the better. Committee discussions are mostly conversational, and you don't even realize when you've begun to join in. Listen carefully and make brief notes. Although you won't always use them, they'll give you confidence and a sense of security. Jennifer's experience with a review panel, actual lingual participation at smaller meetings, soon made her feel ready for the big time.

What to say No longer having an excuse to be still the whole time, Jennifer took the plunge whenever she had an appropriate comment or question.

| *Jennifer:* | "Yes, that experience we had last February points up the danger of..." |
| | "It seems to me the real problem is...I think it's caused by...and this can be corrected if we..." |

2. Speak calmly—don't reveal your anger or annoyance

You know others have as much right to a view as you do. Then let them finish without your interrupting. Your objective is to disagree pleasantly.

> **TIP:** Deliberately lower your voice, and don't let your pride keep you from changing your mind. Practice yielding while you organize your thoughts. Really listen. You may learn something new or modify your view.

Strategy Listen to both sides. Don't be the first to voice an opinion. Waiting will keep you from coming on too strong and you'll often find that your position is better if you're the rebutter.

John was arguing in favor of going after a new group of clients. Kathleen opposed his conclusion and said so. John bristled, but Kathleen quickly calmed him down.

What to say Kathleen knew she'd get further if, before explaining her contradiction, she said something on which they both agreed or if she expressed admiration for one of John's good qualities.

| *John:* | "Kathleen, how can you say that when every study shows that..." |
| *Kathleen:* | "John, let me say first of all that I admire your thoroughness. The research you did..." |

Kathleen got his attention. If you want someone to hear you, don't shout. Instead, start quietly with an honest compliment or a point of agreement.

3. Target the discussions when the chairperson fails to

Your boss is afraid to hurt anyone's feelings. At the weekly meetings, this "leader" can't or won't exercise control. Consequently, the staff complain to each other that the sessions are unproductive with everyone going off on tangents. When a chairperson shirks this responsibility, there's no need to nod agreement with everything said.

> **TIP:** Talk up. Shed some insight others are obviously missing. If you sit back on your harassment in bored silence, resenting colleagues who are petty thinkers, you're not helping yourself or your office. Don't just think big, act big.

Strategy Your objective is to get issues resolved and the tactic is to casually take hold. The skill is not to scold, but to begin as though you are joining in.

Joyce said the staff meetings for her division were important and necessary, but her boss allowed too much time to be wasted with irrelevant personal examples. I suggested she break into the discussion unobtrusively.

What to say Define the pressing problem, the real question, the basic issue.

> **Joyce:** "I know we're all so terribly interested in this subject that we could go on like this for hours. But I think what we really have to decide right now is how we are going to fund the project."

After getting the discussion back on target a few times, Joyce's boss kept turning to her to pick up the cue. Whenever there's a leadership vacuum, someone eventually fills it. If you sense an opportunity to lead your peers, grab it and your boss will be grateful.

4. "Formalize" informal reports

Some people complain no one listens when they report. They have to speak above the buzzing of several private conversations.

Usually complainers admit to winging it, compounding the problem by reading their last-minute scribbling. For short reports as for longer presentations, the objective is to maintain attention.

Strategy

(1) *Take time to prepare.* When delivering a short message there are no words to waste. Instead of waiting until report day to dash it off, jot down ideas while performing routine tasks. Then sift your notes to keep only what's new and worthy, and finally shuffle them to get one thought flowing into the next.

(2) *Look everyone in the eye.* What you say isn't nearly as important as how you say it and how you look. Keep eye contact with the audience to hold their attention. Look down just long enough to glance at the points to be made. Practice at home from this list. If a record of the report is needed, file a copy—*DON'T READ IT.* Also, don't memorize—it's very embarrassing if you get stuck. The exception is to memorize a good opening and closing (discussed more fully in Chapter 3).

(3) *Keep a good pace.* Don't speed up to get it over with or otherwise broadcast nervousness. If you hear yourself "uh" and "um," stop momentarily until you collect your thoughts.

(4) *Give the group a shock treatment.* The unexpected will produce an electrifying effect. Snag interest, for example, with a personalized story. "Yesterday I went to see our client, Garrison Brown, and imagine my surprise when I saw that. . ."

(5) *Lighten up.* You don't want to flip a quip every few seconds, but laugh at yourself when you goof. Poke fun at outmoded rituals the way comedians exaggerate the truth ("How hot was it? It was so hot that. . .")

5. *Dramatize your presentation to spark interest*

When your message is too important to chance an ordinary presentation, try some of these tactics:

(1) *Demonstrate with pictures, posters, and other clarifying visuals.* You don't have to be an artist to manage stick drawings or flow charts on the blackboard.

(2) *Encourage questions from or ask questions to the group.*

> "From your own experience, what do you think it takes to get them to sign up?"

(3) *Create a catchy title for the new project.*

(4) *Employ visuals*—video cassettes, films, film strips, slides, maps, charts and photo exhibits. A dozen sheets of continuous-fold computer paper can dramatize enormity by letting one page represent *x*-amount.

(5) *Consider audio aids*—tape-recorded interviews, musical background tapes, and records.

(6) *Get first-hand accounts*—a worker's experience with the equipment in question or a case history to put people into your purpose.

(7) *Use role-playing* to spotlight particular problems.

(8) *Mount exhibits* on easels or on walls around the room.

(9) *Invite guest experts to speak* (whom you've heard somewhere else first—they may also be expert at putting everyone to sleep).

(10) *Plant a few friends* to ask questions that will encourage a really good discussion after your report.

(11) *Distribute a one-page fact sheet*—a brief, staccato summary. Do this only when you're through. You want them listening to you, not reading it while you're speaking.

Five Techniques to Capture Attention on the Telephone

If awareness training were given to everybody who picks up an office telephone, there wouldn't be nearly as many bad connections. Try recording a few conversations with your peers to spot what you should have left unsaid or might have stated more clearly or concisely. How you use the phone can either capture attention or turn people off. Here are a few unwritten rules.

1. Assure good reception—don't be a telephone pest

If you recognize yourself among any of the following, get your lines uncrossed.

Game players delight in making you waste time. Lisa is in the middle of a meeting and Jim is playing a juvenile guessing game.

Jim: "Hello, Lisa, do you know who this is?"

What to say Right after the greeting, Jim should identify himself rather than assume everybody will recognize his dulcet tones.

And if there are seven Jims on the same floor, he should give both names:

Jim: "Hello, Lisa, this is Jim Black."

Incessant talkers identify themselves but, without coming up for air, launch into their discussion. Marie had just 30 seconds to join the boss at the elevator, but John wouldn't give her a chance to say this.

John: "Marie, this is John, I'm writing a report on the Peterson case and I need. . ."

What to say When you're on the receiving end and in a hurry to scurry, you must interrupt by cutting in and talking over the caller:

Marie: "Excuse me, I'm sorry I can't talk now. I'll call you back."

And John must learn to take a breath and first inquire:

John: "Marie, this is John. Do you have a minute [or two or ten or whatever he needs] to talk to me now?"

Affronters put their victims on the defensive with words and a tone that imply faults such as stupidity or neglect.

Alena: "What do you mean 'What's on Friday?' Don't you ever read the newsletter?"

What to say Of course people resent such treatment and Alena has to improve her manners.

Alena: "Perhaps you're not aware that on Friday we have a fine opportunity to. . ."

Self-appointed screeners take it upon themselves to protect their peers in an annoying way. Although never specifically instructed to screen all calls for subject matter, they'll take the message and ask:

"What's this in regard to?"

What to say   Maybe they mean well, but their trying is prying. It is simply none of their business and many callers are intensely irritated by this practice. Unless otherwise requested, the response is

> "May I have James call you back as soon as he returns?"

Blabbermouths tell every caller more than the caller needs to know. For instance, Hal informs anyone:

> **Hal:**   "Judd can't come to the telephone because he's on a coffee break."
> "Judd never comes in before 10:00 on Thursdays."

What to say   Don't stuff excessive, indiscriminate information into simple message-taking. It's enough to say

> "Judd's away from his desk. May I tell him who called?"

2.   *Strategize before you dial*

In exchange for their time, you owe your colleagues a sharp, meaningful message or a clear, concise interview. Consider that whenever you call, you interrupt someone else.

TIP: Before you dial, remember to smile. Good humor and a pleasant manner come through in the voice. You never know when it's the president of your company or your best customer on the other end, so answer *all* telephone calls in a friendly, conversational tone.

Strategy

 (1) Before you place the call, jot down the points you want to make and the questions to ask.
 (2) Rearrange your list or renumber the items for a logical flow.

Brooke has to elicit a considerable amount of information over the telephone. Her peers are cooperative, but irked that Brooke doesn't ask all her questions at one time, disturbing them at least once or twice more to get additional facts she could have ascertained during the first round.

What to say   Brooke sensed the agitation. She agreed to be more considerate and get her thoughts organized before she dialed.

> ***Brooke:***   "Hi, Debbie. This is Brooke. How are you doing? Good. I'm calling about the dates we need for the new schedule."

With her new system, Brooke got right to the point and usually got all the information she needed from the one original call.

3. Call back even if you don't have the answer

Sometimes you feel compelled to guess at an answer you're not quite ready to give. Since you have to call back anyway to confirm or change, this habit is a waste of everyone's time as well as a possible embarrassment to you.

What to say   A better response is:

> "I have to (think about that) (check that out). May I get back to you (in an hour) (tomorrow) (next week)?"

4. Hang up gracefully—don't prolong the call

When the conversation is obviously over, do you have trouble getting off the phone gracefully and therefore keep talking?

What to say   Practice a few handy closings, such as

> "It was nice talking to you."
>
> "Thanks for (the data) (your help)."
>
> "I have a call on the other line. We'll talk again soon."
>
> "May I call you back when I have more information?"

5. Use the phone when you haven't time to write

Don't leave it unsaid because you didn't have time for a letter or memo. Forget the form and use the phone. Unless you need a written record of specific information, calling is cheaper, faster, eliminates paperwork, and captures attention immediately.

Four Techniques to Capture Attention with Your Voice

Although you deserve a reward for trying to improve, go stand in a corner. Say anything. You'll get an idea of how you actually sound to others as the walls throw back the sound.

> **TIP:** Find a passage from a story or editorial and talk into your trusty tape recorder. Play it back to *really listen* to yourself.

Strategy Check the items you want to work on.

( ) Is your voice monotonous in speed, pitch, or volume?
( ) Does your voice drop at the end of each sentence?
( ) Does your voice rise when you intended no question?
( ) Is there a choppy, erratic rhythm?
( ) Is there a quivering, nervous beat?
( ) Do you run words together, speeding up to get through?
( ) Are you so slow and soft you put everyone to sleep?
( ) Are you ear-piercing loud or shrill?
( ) Are you slurring beginning and endings or mumbling?

Here's how to overcome many of these negative traits.

1. Practice daily voice drills

If your face, neck, and throat muscles are tense, this can cause a shrill pitch, and at times makes you appear to be uncontrolled and overemotional. Stop straining your vocal cords as well as your friends' tolerance. Begin a daily routine of exercises to help you relax your muscles and benefit from better inhaling and exhaling.

Lynn has been uncomfortable and self-conscious about her voice ever since the time she overheard someone describe her as

"The one with the high-pitched voice. It's like being serenaded by fingernails scraped across a blackboard."

What helped Lynn? Her exercises included

- deep breathing from the diaphragm
- yawning, inhaling through the nose with the mouth open slightly, and releasing air through the mouth in small, steady streams
- sticking out the tongue and holding for a few seconds.
- scrunching together the whole face, holding, relaxing, and reversing with a wide grin
- rolling the head slowly from left to right and right to left

Lynn also practiced lowering her voice so that her messages would be better received. In a short time, she was down a half-octave. This is the procedure she followed.

(1) Relax in a comfortable chair, feet firmly on the floor

(2) Read a short sentence into your tape recorder

(3) Let your chin rest on your chest and read it again

(4) Sit up straight and concentrate on your voice being relaxed and lower as you again read and record the sentence

Another drill is to practice emulating professional radio and TV announcers. Notice how they

- change inflection without resorting to extremes
- round out vowels—their voices never sound flat
- they sound out consonants precisely
- utilize their voices to enrich the meaning (on TV, notice their faces curving up to express pleasure or to question; curving down when sad)
- keep their tone conversational

2. *Scrutinize your expressions and mannerisms*

> **TIP:** Study your mannerisms in the mirror as you have a conversation with yourself. Analyze facial expressions in your unposed photos to help you determine how you are coming across.

Tape-record a conversation with a friend or the family *to hear the manner you use* in discussions. Some people are flabbergasted to learn how preachy and dogmatic they can be. Others are astonished at the length of time they remain silent, unable to interrupt to get a word in. Some hear themselves get excited, and speak so rapidly that their words are hard to distinguish.

As you listen to yourself, notice if you are going beyond "I," "my," and "mine." Your listeners are much more impressed if you stress "you," "your" and "yours."

3. Select the clearest and most appropriate word

Choose the simpler word if it says the same thing as the more complex one. But at times the longer word is the wiser choice because it conveys a better shade of meaning, as in:

Simple: "The swimmers used the same strokes at the same time."

Better: "The swimmers synchronized their strokes."

The point is appropriateness. Look up exact, precise meanings in the dictionary as part of your everyday routine. Use more fitting descriptive terms and more exciting verbs, adjectives, and adverbs. "Sweltering" paints a better picture than "very hot and humid"; the specific "Great Dane" creates a clearer image than the general term "large dog."

TIP: Talk as one human being to another. You're not a machine nor an administrative order. Sound alive. Police reports may require a stilted "The perpetrator was apprehended at 14:00" type of formality. But for you to keep attention, convert jargon into everyday words. "Ascertain" translates to "find out"; procure. . .get; render. . .give; in view of the above. . .since; the committee is of the opinion that. . .we believe.

---

4. Be explicit and decisive

When you enunciate clearly, others perceive you as controlled or authoritative. If enunciation is a problem, add tongue twisters to your practice sessions. Make sure you aren't mumbling "com-ere," "Ispose" and "whatcha wan."

Review your taped discussions listening for statements or questions indicating indecisiveness or meekness. When a situation requires a strong assertion, eliminate the soft "I feel" or "I believe" that weakens it.

Accept a resolution the group has reached without rehashing the matter ("Shouldn't we talk this over some more?") You had your chance, they already heard you.

If you frequently "er" and "um" or dot your sentences with "ya know, ya know," concentrate on closing your mouth until you can collect your thoughts.

There's no substitute for experience in order to become more comfortable and effective when talking to your colleagues—in conversations, group discussions or on the phone. Keep recording your practice sessions so that you can *hear for yourself* how you're coming across. With enough practice, you'll get and keep attention whenever you speak to colleagues.

PART THREE

What to Say to the People Who Work for You

CHAPTER 11

$$\boxed{}$$

Four Sure-Fire Ways to Nurture Loyalty from Your Staff

QUIZ #11. HOW LOYAL IS YOUR STAFF?

Choose the answer to each question that best fits your situation. The interpretation of your choices follows.

1. The emotional climate in your office is

   (a) predictably harmonious
   (b) tightly controlled
   (c) encourages critical comments

2. Before asking your staff for suggestions, you

   (a) say the best suggestions will be considered
   (b) imply the best suggestions will be used
   (c) promise the best suggestions will be used

3. After your staff has come up with suggestions, you

   (a) promise to take them to your boss—eventually
   (b) request they reduce their ideas to writing
   (c) feel you needn't report your boss's reaction to your staff

4. In giving directions to subordinates, you

    (a) depend on facial expressions and gestures

    (b) spell out what you mean to convey

    (c) ask workers to restate them in their own words

5. When it comes to goals and objectives, you tell your staff

    (a) the company and unit aims

    (b) to develop objectives in line with the company's and unit's objectives

    (c) you'll help them write their objectives

6. To improve job performance, you

    (a) frequently make specific comments

    (b) offer to help after the worker does something wrong

    (c) accept or reject sloppy workmanship depending on the reason

7. When a blunder occurs in your unit, you

    (a) explain it wasn't your fault; you didn't know about it

    (b) shoulder the blame, no matter who was at fault

    (c) promise to catch the culprit

8. When you delegate tasks to subordinates, you

    (a) maintain rigid control to guard against error

    (b) delegate only easy tasks where error is unlikely

    (c) allow them to make mistakes

9. You tell those working under your subordinates

    (a) to go first to their supervisor who'll come to you if necessary

    (b) to go first to their supervisors, then to you

    (c) come directly to you, bypassing their supervisor

10. Your idea of adding a personal touch is to

    (a) use competition, prizes, and special award programs

    (b) send each employee a printed Christmas card

    (c) distribute ten-year service pins

Interpretation

1.   Unless workers are free to express, question and disagree, it's your unit, not theirs. Tight control and continuous harmony don't instill loyalty.

2.   You mislead if you imply or promise the best suggestions will be used. All you can promise and all they should expect is for the idea to be considered.

3.   Their loyalty erodes if you don't keep your promise or report back. Getting ideas in writing sharpens their thinking and reminds you to act.

4.   When subordinates feel you truly want them to do well, you build lasting loyalty. The message from (a) is indifference; (b) may be insufficient; (c) meets their needs.

5.   Neither (a) or (b) meshes their personal goals with company/unit goals. Helping them produce clear, dated, measurable objectives increases their allegiance.

6.   They won't trust you if you're inconsistent or wait to catch them. Give professional, caring feedback immediately, specifying what's wrong and how to improve it.

7.   Subordinates feel loyal and respect leaders strong enough to own up to blunders in their unit and smart enough to prevent it from recurring.

8.   Both (a) and (b) are stifling. By freeing them to make mistakes and learn through new situations, you show your faith in their capabilities.

9.   You, too, must obey the chain of command. If you don't give your assistants this support and respect, why should they be loyal to you?

10.   Make work more enjoyable. Managers who show showmanship by utilizing competition usually have devoted followers and productive workers.

HOW TO INSPIRE PERSONAL DEDICATION FROM YOUR TEAM

You've tried to develop loyalty to the company because if your workers don't believe in what they're doing, you may as well give up. Instead of selling the company, they won't perform well or will be constantly bickering.

Tell them how their personal goals (security, prestige, achievement, and so on) dovetail with company goals. You give them a sense of accomplishment, explaining that even the most routine job is an important peg in the whole operation. All workers want to feel their being there makes some difference.

At the same time, you want to develop their loyalty to you. By offering to share the planning, problems, and progress, you demonstrate you are there for each other and that your subordinates are important to you. Even if they are a little short on devotion to the department, if they're dedicated to you, their leader, that's a solid motivational footing. Without it, your unit can be unbalanced. And the larger the unit, the louder the crash if the walls come tumbling down.

Try these four ways to plant and nourish personal loyalty.

- Make yourself accessible to complaints
- Be perfectly clear about what you expect from your staff
- Give motivating feedback
- Add fun, flair, and style to your directives

Make Yourself Accessible to Complaints

When you're feeling smug because you've heard no complaints, that's the time to worry. It's human nature to gripe. But to bring up a problem, your people have to know you allow respectful disagreement. Show your interest, open your door, and establish set times such as every morning 8:00-9:00 A.M. or Friday afternoons after 2:00 P.M. when you are available for feedback.

Glean important information from hostile comments

For you to succeed, you need your workers to succeed. *Only through them* do you achieve the results you want. Therefore, instead of seeking a win/lose solution, go for a win/win outcome, something everyone can feel good about. You're not worth your salt unless you allow and listen to the peppery comments of hostile workers. What are you afraid of—a little progress? Your objective is to maintain enthusiasm at a high level.

> **TIP:** Remembering to talk to subordinates you promised to get back to shows you care and eliminates resentment. Whether your entries are on huge desk pads or small daily calendars or "Talk to...Date...Regarding" sheets, have some set procedure for follow-up talks.

Strategy

    (1) Talk in an open, conciliatory manner to subordinates with whom you're at loggerheads.

    (2) Design and adhere to a system that keeps everyone informed of latest developments.

Kevin had had several screaming confrontations with Bart, his production chief, and knew he had to try another tactic. Yelling wasn't working.

What to say   Kevin acknowledged that he needed a direct, nonconfrontational "What's bothering you? Let's talk about it" approach.

> ***Kevin:***   "Bart, I know you're angry. I truly want to hear what you have to say about the new system. Don't pull any punches."
>
> ***Bart:***   "Kevin, your new method is terrible. It's slowing us down far too much. The only way it could work is to alter the..."
>
> ***Kevin:***   "Thanks, Bart. That idea deserves careful consideration. I will get back to you as soon as I can. By Friday for sure, so keep cool."

The result was a compromise that both agreed was an improvement. More importantly, this established the pattern of a boss willing to hear opposing opinions.

How to respond after a blow up

Being accessible and open lets you defuse and often solve problems before they escalate. If you don't discuss a problem, your subordinates bottle up their frustrations until they explode. Your *objective* is to help your employees become productive again.

> **TIP:** People who take pride in their work need to get satisfaction by expressing their ideas on how to improve quality and procedures. If denied this opportunity, their hostility grows and you lose out on good ideas.

Strategy

    (1) Stay calm and let irate workers get it off their chests

    (2) Soothe wounded feelings by working with them on the problem

    (3) Point out the mutual benefits to your helping them.

Bart wasn't the only contender for the title of discontent employee. Kevin told me he felt like he'd been hit by a tornado when Chris, his assistant, blew his stack.

> **Chris:** "This place stinks. You aren't supposed to use your mind. You use a procedure manual to tell you what to say, when to say it, what to do, and even what to feel. And don't dare feel anything else or the whole company is thrown out of whack. I'm wasting my time on this job."

What to say   This needed a calm and caring response.

> **Kevin:** "Chris, you're obviously at the end of your rope. You know we all appreciate the fine work you do, and if you're tied up in red tape, let's untangle it.
> "Of course we're here to make money, but it's also vital you feel good about your work. When you're more productive, there's more profit which, in turn, pays for our raises and greater security. We're all going up on the same elevator. Now what can we do to straighten things out?"

Remember, your workers wouldn't get so hot under the collar if they didn't care. Let them know you're playing on the same team.

How to ask your people for their ideas

Periodically, get away from your desk to talk to people in the field for information independent of what your top lieutenants feed you. You'll stop hailing the status quo and start listening to new ideas and better ways to do things.

Your objective is to let your staff know you want to consider their suggestions affecting their work and to create a climate that encourages such contributions. If you don't ask, they won't offer. They may think you'll resent their ideas or that they'll look foolish or uninformed.

TIP: Reinforce your request to hear their ideas. Offer prizes, rewards or recognition for the best suggestions. Invite a different small group of your staff to lunch with you every couple of weeks to fill them in on new happenings affecting the company and to listen to their concerns. This is an excellent way to get good feedback. You may also hold regularly scheduled weekly staff meetings at which you solicit solutions for specific problems.

Strategy   Establish the ground rules.

1.   Ask for their succinct, specific ideas in writing. Explain that seeing their ideas on paper sharpens their thoughts and helps them spot potential problems. This also gives you a tangible reminder to take upstairs.

2.   Tell them their recommendations are suggestions to be considered and you really want to hear them. They may or may not be accepted, but each one will be carefully reviewed and you'll let them know the result.

3.   Promise to alert your boss to any suggestions that encompass other departments, and that you'll be sure to credit the source of the idea.

Eleanor did everything right when she openly asked for her subordinates' ideas and arranged a meeting to discuss them. Her staffers excitedly came up with concrete suggestions. But it backfired because Eleanor dropped the ball. Follow up is as important in responding to employee suggestions as it is with employee problems. Later, Eleanor heard comments like this:

JoAnn: "Eleanor, I believe I was sloughed off. You never told me the reaction of the front office to my idea."

What to say   Eleanor knew it would be more difficult for her to elicit suggestions next time unless she dealt with the situation honestly.

> **Eleanor:** "I'm sorry, JoAnn. It was my fault that I failed to report your good suggestion. To prevent this mistake from recurring, from now on we'll follow a new procedure: (1)... (2)... (3)..."

It's not enough to ask your subordinates for their ideas, you also need to spell out your procedures for considering them.

Be Perfectly Clear About What You Expect from Your Staff

As the dramatist Geothe wrote, where we stand isn't as important as the direction in which we're moving. Your workers need to know exactly where *you* are moving—and in which direction you're headed—before they have confidence in the boss they're to follow.

Give precise directions

If your people aren't doing what you've told them to do, take a hard look at the way you're giving directions.

> **TIP:** Say what you mean to convey. Don't depend on facial expressions or gestures that can be misinterpreted or seem to contradict your words.

Now take the following steps:

(1) *Spell out the details in writing for the tasks to be accomplished and each person's duties.* Clearly define the goals, responsibilities, lines of authority, manpower, equipment, money, materials, deadlines, and whatever else is required.

(2) *State your directions in plain English with each employee.* Level with them about exact deadlines to avoid constant checking. In a tone that denotes authority and understanding, tell them what's involved, why they're equipped to do it, and why you think they'd want to.

Candice: "I want you to handle the Stapleton matter. I know
Mrs. Stapleton has been a pain, but you're the best
presenter I have and this will give you a chance to
develop your research skills."

(3) *Invite their questions and then ask them to restate the
directions* you've given to make sure they understand.

Spell out measurable performance objectives to build allegiance

This combined verbal/written approach also works well when
you want to set performance goals for the staff in your department.

TIP: Agree in advance on what is expected. When the assignment is completed, you need a reference that plainly tells
you if the goals were achieved. Your objective is to agree on
the *gauge* both you and your subordinate will use to judge
how well that subordinate is performing.

Strategy Plan along with your staff rather than plead with or
threaten them.

(1) Ask each employee to develop his or her own performance
goals to get them involved in the decisions that affect
them.
(2) Explain how to develop an objective, including dates by
which specific tasks will be completed. "By June 1st, I will
have produced 75 widgets."
(3) Follow up in writing so that both boss and worker have
the same written document to refer to if questions arise.

LuAnn was faced with a ten percent increase as part of her
company's goal for the coming year. She called her workers into
her office, one at a time, to talk about goals and objectives.

What to say When Stuart objected to putting his goals in writing, LuAnn explained how to go about setting an objective.

LuAnn: "Don't panic, Stuart. Instead of saying *generally*
that you'll improve coverage, be specific. You al-

ready know how many contacts you are now making and what percent results in stories. Just figure how many more contacts you'd have to make a month to reach your goal of a ten percent increase. For example, if you now make 50, increase your contacts by ten percent to 55. Then we'll negotiate a reasonable workload."

Stuart begrudgingly complied, but later told LuAnn he really liked having measurable objectives because he always knew where he stood. Stated objectives increase subordinate loyalty.

How to reject poor work by matching it with written goals

You can enforce excellent standards and still be well liked. Besides giving precise directions and helping your subordinates state well-defined objectives, you also have to be direct and sensitive when accepting and rejecting work turned in to you.

TIP: Openly discuss your expectations and return anything that's sub-standard. If you accept sloppy workmanship, you will continue to be given sloppy work.

Strategy Your objective is to help your employees reach and maintain a high level of performance. Be consistent in your expectation and tactfully refuse to accept any work that is not up to *your* standards.

Jimmy is a boss who wants everyone to like him. Therefore, when work isn't up to par, Jimmy always asks his assistant to correct it instead of sending the work back to the individual. As a result, some of his staff take advantage of his vulnerability. Jimmy also has a habit of apologizing for giving difficult assignments and then finds it hard to order that the work be redone.

What to say To avoid resentment, Jimmy practiced stating ways to say that he knows the worker wants to do better. For example:

> **Jimmy:** "Ira, I've marked the sections that aren't clear or that need documentation. I'm sure you'll want to correct them."

By being consistent about the quality he deemed acceptable, Jimmy gained new respect from his team. The more you expect, the more you get, especially if what you expect was mutually agreed upon in advance and you remain firm.

Give Motivating Feedback

Good feedback is specific, given as soon as possible, and presented in a professional, non-threatening manner. Your *objective* in giving feedback is to assist your subordinates and encourage them to talk about their assignments.

TIP: Tell your subordinates you know you can depend on them to come through. When they feel you're counting on them, they try harder.

Strategy

(1) Reassure them you have confidence in their skills.

(2) Make it appear easy for them to accomplish the desired improvements.

Russ thought he understood what Mac had told him to do until midway, when he checked his progress. Mac managed to demoralize Russ without giving him a single clue as to how to improve his original effort.

Mac: "Oh, this is bad, Russ. You're going to have to do it again. I thought when I gave you this job, I could count on you to come through for me. I certainly didn't anticipate this kind of mumbo jumbo. I expect a good draft this time next week."

What to say Mac had to spell out what he wanted from Russ. I suggested that he offer constructive, specific suggestions.

Mac: "Russ, you've got some good information here, but the purpose of this piece is to motivate. I think it's too heavy. I've marked some paragraphs for us to discuss. How do you feel about switching. . .?"

It's not only important to be specific, it's also vital to have a good *tone* when giving feedback. More than what you say, it's how you say it, if you are going to inspire loyalty.

Correcting mistakes on delegated work

Mistakes provide the opportunity to grow. The freedom to handle responsibility isn't worth a hoot without the freedom to make mistakes. If you let your subordinates experiment with a better way, as long as it is within the framework of your rules, even if they make mistakes, they'll learn from them. You can't be certain the work you delegate will be error-free, but that's the price of progress.

The art of delegating balances requirements of the task with capabilities of the person chosen to do it, and then backing off. As Teddy Roosevelt advised executives, have enough sense to pick good men to do the job and enough self restraint not to meddle with them while they do it.

TIP: Examine your own delegating pattern if you're feeling overworked. Make sure you aren't hanging on to a task you know you should give up. Sometimes we simply enjoy doing something and refuse to let it go.

Once you delegate, you have to deal with subordinates who make errors that have to be rectified. The *objective* is to resolve the trouble with criticism that instills, not kills, the spirit to try harder. Yell and threaten enough and anyone will tune you out.

Strategy

(1) Stress the need for results that have to be achieved instead of emphasizing each detailed step to achieve them.

(2) Install controls, such as periodic progress reports, that let you catch major blunders before they occur. Be reasonable—don't hamper your staff, requiring them to get signature approvals at seven different levels of management.

Vince, reluctant to delegate, failed to show confidence in his subordinates. He checked up on their every act and decision and his unasked-for advice was having an adverse "why should I try?" effect. It was only after he recognized their disinterest and half-hearted efforts that he accepted the need to be tactfully helpful.

What to say   Enable your staff to figure some things out for themselves.

> ***Vince:*** "Hank, I know you can handle this. Here's a folder with the information you'll need. If you run into trouble, let me know. I'll be anxious to read your weekly reports."

By supplying the guidelines, telling when and how to report and then backing off, Vince allowed Hank to learn to anticipate difficulties. Let your subordinates resolve some problems and grow in the process.

How to correct the new worker

Another supervisory headache occurs with new people who come with great rave notices. Although you review procedures with them, nothing turned in is the way you want it or need it. This type of new worker has his or her own system and doesn't bother to check with anyone.

TIP: Observe newcomers closely. Having experience elsewhere won't necessarily produce what you want. They may be experienced—in doing it wrong.

In areas where conforming to your procedures is essential, your *objective* is to make the new worker understand that nothing less is acceptable.

Strategy

(1) Be firm, but tactful. Wait until your anger cools before speaking.
(2) Emphasize the importance of following rules, and the consequences if they're not followed. Document this talk for possible future action.
(3) End on a note of encouragement.

Marcus was happy to welcome Jackie whose good reputation preceded her and carefully explained that they had to have certain appraisal estimates on Tuesday. When Tuesday came, all Jackie gave him was an excuse. Marcus could only take his lumps and apologize to his boss for the embarrassing delay.

What to say Marcus was seething but delayed the confrontation until he composed himself.

Marcus: "Jackie, I realize we do things a little differently here. But you knew we were committed to have those estimates this morning. Not being ready puts all our jobs in jeopardy. Study your manual. I'm depending on you not to let this mistake happen again. Show me the excellent work I know you are capable of doing."

While new workers need special understanding and support, they also need a firm hand to learn to do things your way.

How to coach without encroaching

Ideally, a supervisor/coach gives precise directions, then lets the worker figure out how to accomplish the task. If the worker is stuck, instead of telling, ask questions (How long would you estimate? What would you need in order to. . .?) And then if you have to tell, suggest (Wouldn't it be better if we. . .?)

TIP: Give your subordinates the chance to solve their own problems. Qualified workers who sit on a thorny problem usually rise to the challenge. Your aim is to have your staff work independently. They're not learning if they're leaning on you.

Strategy Manage by exception. Give your staff breathing room by telling them:

(1) To come to you only with something unusual or a problem they can't solve.
(2) To feel free to come to you because resolving a difficult situation is a mutual learning experience.

Norm admitted he'd lost faith in his department. He revealed to me that his staff members know what's expected, yet he makes calls they were to make and prepares reports they were to write. One day he overheard his assistant Larry comment to the others:

Larry: "The boss believes he's the only one who can do it. Norm can do it better. Norm can do it faster. Norm is so anxious to have something to crow about, he insists on pecking at each job himself."

Norm was hurt, but he saw himself then as his crew saw him. A few had already transferred to another department.

What to say   Norm agreed to stop intruding on his subordinates' space, but he also had to discourage them from hiding errors.

> **Norm:**   "We all make mistakes. When you goof up, we'll review it so we can both do a better job."

Compulsive doing or checking makes a boss a flop at the top. Once Norm stopped henpecking, he had happier workers plus more free time to think about the total operation.

Expressing support instead of going over a worker's head

Even though you allow your subordinates to tend their own trees, with hands off unless they get stumped, you still must obey the chain of command.

TIP: Aid, don't invade.

Strategy   Do your job and let your assistants do theirs. Express respect for their competence. They need and deserve your support. Your objective is to assist, not belittle, your assistants.

Marsha is a new division director trying hard to have everything run smoothly. One of her unit heads, Terry, was upset because a project director under Terry's domain had a problem, called Marsha, and Marsha immediately suggested how it should be handled. Terry complained that Marsha wasn't being supportive and loyal to her officers.

> **Marsha:**   "But Terry, how can I refuse to help anyone who comes to me?"
>
> **Terry:**   "By referring her back to me. Helping project directors is my job."

What to say   Even though Terry works under Marsha, Marsha went over Terry's head. The department director saw her error. The next time a project coordinator came to her, she handled the situation differently.

Marsha: "I appreciate your concern, but I think you should start by calling Terry. If there's still a problem, your boss Terry will tell me about it."

Marsha reinforced respect for Terry by placing responsibility where it belonged. And in doing so, she strengthened the loyalty ties.

Add Fun, Flair, and Style to Your Directives

Show your showmanship. It's no sin to enjoy work and put life into the daily routine. An exhilarated leader is magnetic. If management doesn't understand the importance of having fun, they may be making everyone lackadaisical.

Set your unit's mood and pace

Send the message that your baliwick is a pleasant place. As the manager, your style and tone permeate the air.

TIP: What you say to subordinates speeds up or slows down the pace. Your *objective* is to find a comfortable, but challenging rate that keeps the atmosphere calm and free of constant anxiety.

Strategy Guide those who go over or under that rate. Ease up when the group is tired ("Why don't we call it a day?") and let them catch their collective breaths. Control anyone exerting undue pressure.

Cloe is a classic workhorse who's always last to leave and often takes work home. Jill, who supervises her, was concerned that (1) she'll burn out, and (2) she makes everyone tense. To harness Cloe's energy, Jill agreed to enforce her rules.

Jill: "Cloe, everybody leaves by 5:30—no exceptions without my personal authorization."

When Cloe, as usual, was the first to offer help, Jill began gently and politely to turn her down.

> ***Jill:***   "Thanks a million, Cloe, but I already have the help I need."

Once Cloe was subdued, the office calmed down. It takes only one person pushing too hard to get everyone else on edge, so if you direct a workhorse, tighten the reins. Maintain a challenging, but genial, mood and pace.

Use verbal showmanship to gain involvement

Showmanship is developing an effective style or flair that generates interest and excitement. It's not so much what you say, but how you say it. It's your way of involving everyone at every level in what's going on.

> **TIP:** Make it possible for each one to say what he or she thinks by creating a friendly environment. Your objective is to make your subordinates feel that it's "their" company or department, or organization.

Strategy

(1) Know when to substitute a human instead of an academic approach or a display for a discourse.

(2) Dare to be different by using games or gimmicks to point up problems or help workers identify and pull together.

Carla was contemplating how to assemble her team to perform the boring task of stuffing and sealing envelopes for a special mailing that *had* to get out on time.

What to say   Make it sound enjoyable.

> ***Carla:***   "You are expected to attend a coffee at 3:00 P.M. that will appeal to your love for loquacity. While sealing envelopes, there's many a quip 'twixt the lick and the lip."

Set up contests to inject enthusiasm, divide work and conquer apathy

When you ask for help, is it always the same few who always volunteer? You can spread extra assignments more evenly with a little system to divide the work and conquer the apathy.

> **TIP:** Try friendly rivalry. It's fun and catching. The task isn't a grind if you make it a game.

Strategy Use a competitive approach. Define ground rules, prizes, and other incentives promoting extra work as a contest. For the prize to be an incentive, it has to be something the worker doesn't have or isn't likely to get.

What to say Get them excited.

> "Ok, gang, we're going to divide the unit into three teams. Ed, Gini, and Whitley will be captains. Members of the team that logs the most hours will be given extra leave time, and the person with the highest amount gets a weekend trip..."

People often work harder for a small group with which they identify than they will for themselves. When they're working as part of a team, they are often inspired more by loyalty to their group and desire for group success than they are by the prize being offered.

There's no match for enthusiasm to light a fire under your workers, but you're fingered as a phony if you don't feel it yourself. Above all, it is your own sincerity and concern for your staff, both as individuals and as members of your team, that ignites the feelings of loyalty you hope they feel for you.

CHAPTER 12

```
  _____
 (                      )
  ‾‾‾‾‾‾‾‾‾‾‾‾‾‾‾‾‾‾‾‾‾‾
```

How to Motivate
a Demoralized Crew

QUIZ #12. DO YOU EXPRESS CONCERN FOR YOUR STAFF?

In both big and little ways, messages you send your subordinates either motivate or demoralize them. A "no" answer to any of these questions pinpoints a potential troublespot for you.

	YES	NO
1. Do you watch reactions and listen to their words to figure out what makes each person tick?	( )	( )
2. Do you ask them about their personal goals?	( )	( )
3. Do you assign challenging tasks to help workers develop their potential?	( )	( )
4. Do you demonstrate your pleasure at their success?	( )	( )
5. Do you provide workshops and other opportunities for development—both as team members and individuals?	( )	( )
6. Do you express your trust and refrain from nagging?	( )	( )

7. Do you give straightforward messages that aren't likely to be misinterpreted? ( ) ( )

8. Do you praise all attempts, even those that failed? ( ) ( )

9. Do you issue praise quickly and graciously in front of their peers? ( ) ( )

10. Do you speak patiently and kindly when rejecting an idea? ( ) ( )

11. Do you frequently give feedback on performance? ( ) ( )

12. Do you often keep your office door open? ( ) ( )

13. Do you regularly schedule staff meetings or small get-togethers? ( ) ( )

14. Do you correct workers privately, not through critical memos or in front of others? ( ) ( )

15. Do you explain and carry out your system for rewarding accomplishment? ( ) ( )

16. Do you hold your calls when conferring with a staff person? ( ) ( )

17. Do you have a system to elicit creative staff solutions for specific company problems? ( ) ( )

18. Do you avoid asking their opinions when you've obviously made up your mind and won't change it? ( ) ( )

19. Do you have a good system to keep them updated? ( ) ( )

20. Do you transmit your staff's thinking for higher management review? ( ) ( )

21. Do you share credit, not hogging it for yourself? ( ) ( )

HOW TO UPLIFT MORALE AMONG DEMOTIVATED WORKERS

The ancient philosopher Plutarch told about a young fellow who got divorced. When astonished friends wanted to know why he'd left such a beautiful and charming woman, the man responded holding out his shoe: "Isn't it new and well made? Yet none of you can tell where it pinches me."

You can't assume that you know what anyone else is feeling and some subordinates won't tell you. But you can resurrect sagging spirits. The symptoms are easy to recognize: morale is low, productivity and team spirit have plummeted, you're facing costly turnovers, employees have quit, the ones who stay are making mistakes, and don't show up or are chronically late. Intentionally and unintentionally, your troops are sabotaging you and your operation.

Besides loss to the business, the subtle hits they score can puncture your career. You never connect them with keeping you from getting it all together—the promotion you don't get, the rejection of your latest proposal, the loss of important papers, broken equipment, missing parts and absenteeism.

If this is your trouble, figure that at the going rate, an ounce of genuine concern will bring you more than a pound of pleading. To keep up the spirits of your subordinates and uplift their morale, send the right message with these three tactics.

- Express genuine concern for the individual
- Express a real appreciation for effort
- Express a true desire to consider their thinking

Express Genuine Concern for the Individual

Everyone has individual likes and dislikes. You turn up your nose at turnips; your friend thinks they're a tempting treat. Or, as Emerson expressed it, "We boil at different degrees." You need to be aware of your employees interests, preferences and limitations. Showing a little concern goes a long way.

Speak honestly—pretending to care is a hazard to your corporate health

Pretending to care can be more hazardous to corporate health than not caring at all. Your objective is to communicate with crystal clarity that you truly care about your people.

TIP: Be sincere when offering help and expressing concern for your subordinates or you may find their resentment building as they devise various ways to get even.

Strategy

    (1) Examine the manner in which you've been talking to detect any insensitivity or insincerity, and

    (2) Transform any phoniness to genuine friendliness.

I know one boss, Albert, who just goes through the motions of caring when actually he considers his staff to be pawns he can manipulate. When he tries to motivate by being personal, he comes out insincere. For example, he has his secretary select and send out Christmas and birthday greetings for his staff—but he doesn't take the time to write a personal note or even sign his own name! Albert gives frequent pep talks, but is never available when his people come to him with problems.

As a result, some workers began faking illnesses, got careless with their work, and took longer lunches. As you can guess, when the monthly figures came in, they were well below the stated goals. Albert knew his job was on the line if he didn't make some fast changes in the way he dealt with his staff. His verbal abuses were common gossip around the office.

What to say   I gave him a basic three-part "Say This, Not That" Plan For Showing Genuine Concern.

    (1) *Promise assistance and give it.* Albert never gave Sandy the help he pledged, but saddled her with all the blame when things went wrong.

> **Albert:** "Sandy, I am holding you personally responsible for our losing that account."

Albert had to own up to his own neglect and turn it into a lesson for both of them.

> **Albert:** "Sandy, I apologize for not giving you the assistance I promised. Maybe we can get back that account if we..."

    (2) *Reprimand in private and correct constructively.* Albert lit into Howard in front of Howard's staff who were even more embarrassed than their boss.

> **Albert:** "Howard, that was a stupid way to handle the complaint. You'll never get anywhere in this organization."

Albert agreed that he had to control his temper and vowed to be more considerate of his subordinates' feelings, using a better approach such as

Albert: "Howard, since the client is our prime concern, do you think there's another way we can handle that complaint without upsetting Mrs. Pesty?"

(3) *Verify your facts and if you're wrong, apologize.* Albert moved on bad information given him by another assistant, but he lunged at Liz for the mistake.

Albert: "Liz, you've got the facts all screwed up. Next time double-check before you hand me a report."

Albert realized he had to take the time to be sure before sounding off, and then he had to temper his remarks. Above all, once Albert saw it was his error, he had to admit it quickly and graciously.

Albert: "Liz, I'm so very sorry both for yelling at you and for accusing you unjustly. Please forgive me. Now about that report. . ."

In communicating with your staff, keep in mind that a subordinate is a friend, not an enemy.

How to send straightforward messages

One of the reasons for expressing your concern is to build trust, but trust is a two-way effort that a boss and subordinate have to work at. If you want your staff to have confidence in you, it is important that you speak clearly, especially when issuing directives. After being given an assignment, subordinates shouldn't have to wonder if you want it done now or later. Nor should they be trying to read something into your raised eyebrow or tapping fingers or ponder if your "Really?" was said sarcastically.

TIP: Be up front with your people. Beware that you might, unintentionally, be sending subordinates mixed messages. For example, automatically saying "Good work" to a subordinate and then writing on the work performance evaluation form critical comments on how that worker must improve.

Your *objective* is to state your requests simply and directly so that everyone knows what you want, when you want it and in what form, as in:

> "Andy, by 9 AM tomorrow I need a summary of the conference that covers A, B, and C."

Verbalize your interest in the feelings of your staff

Expressing concern means freeing your staff to verbalize what they're feeling—even if what they are feeling is hostility toward you. Only by permitting them to express themselves can you both begin to cope with a sticky situation. Your *objective* is to enable your subordinates to talk to you.

TIP: Make sure you haven't been backing your subordinates into a corner. To make it possible for them to feel unconstrained, examine the manner in which you've been talking to them.

Strategy

(1) Allow your subordinates to make the decisions they're supposed to make.
(2) Ask their opinions only when you really want to hear them.
(3) Listen to their ideas, hear them out.

Carole was not aware that she had a penchant for making her people feel trapped. She interfered with the way they assigned their staff and with other decisions that they should have been able to make on their own. She finally came around to seeing the situation from their point of view when she admitted that it takes nerve to stand up to a boss whose mind is definitely made up.

What to say Here are a few examples of how she used to talk to her subordinates and how she learned to say the same thing showing more regard for the feelings of her staff.

(1) Insensitive: "Lee, you have to put another of your people on the Miller deal."

> ***More sensitive:*** "Lee, what about putting another of your people on the Miller deal?"
>
> **(2) *Insensitive:*** "Patty, we have a real problem here. We can either ask for an extension or give a good excuse for the shortage. I think we should ask for an extension."
>
> ***More sensitive:*** "Patty, do you think we should ask for an extension or is there some other way?"
>
> **(3) *Insensitive:*** "Rudy, you know we've tried that before and it won't work. Why are you bringing it up again?"
>
> ***More sensitive:*** "Rudy, how does this differ from what we've done before?"

Being considerate of your subordinates' feelings is an important morale booster.

How to sound fair and avoid the appearance of favoritism

Your subordinates may feel hurt and resentful over simple acts you never imagined were upsetting them and, in particular, if they think you are playing favorites. Your aim is to offer each member of your team equal access to your time.

> **TIP:** It needn't be true that you have favorites. The reality doesn't count as long as your staff perceive that you have favorites to whom you give special treatment.

Strategy Invite all your subordinates to join you periodically out of your office setting. Don't limit yourself to fraternizing with one or two.

Katey and Jayne have been friends for years. Katey was recently promoted and became Jayne's boss, but they still have lunch together almost every day. The other staff members believe that Katey gives Jayne special privileges. She doesn't. But it doesn't matter. They all believe that Jayne gets the choicest accounts and extra time to work on them.

What to say   To deal with Katey's morale problem, I suggested she first explain her predicament to Jayne and then talk to all of her staff.

> **Katey:** "As you know, I eat lunch almost every day at Circle Inn. Any time you want to join me, I'd really be delighted to have your company. So don't be shy. Also, what do you think about our having a monthly outing some place where we can eat and talk business in a more relaxed setting?"

Morale improved considerably after Katey instituted monthly luncheon meetings that were held away from the office in various informal settings.

Express Real Appreciation for Effort

According to renowned psychologist William James, the most fiendish punishment possible is being turned loose in society and remaining absolutely unnoticed. Everybody craves attention. Satisfy this craving. Proclaim your appreciation for the effort your people put forth.

Communicate without middlemen—say it yourself

Whether you are being critical or complimentary, if you depend on those down the chain of command to deliver your sensitive communique, it may get distorted or watered down in the transmission and demoralize your team. Your *objective* is to maintain or re-establish good morale by conveying your appreciation for effort expended, regardless of outcome.

> **TIP:** It is good manners and good business to act as though another person is as important as you are—even if that person is your subordinate. Communicate both congratulatory messages and criticism directly, not through a third party. Place your own phone calls or at least be on the line when the ring is answered. Leave your office occasionally to walk over to your subordinates' desks for brief chats.

Strategy   Be both gracious and sagacious in deciding which messages require your personal delivery. Speak for yourself when what you have to say will be meaningful and motivating to your workers.

John was extremely pleased with the way Abby managed to garner an enormous amount of support from numerous agencies. He told Stacey, his assistant, to congratulate Abby for him but the enthusiasm and appreciation were diluted in the process.

> ***Stacey:***   "Abby, the boss said you did well on that agency assignment."

Abby's disappointment that she didn't get more acknowledgment from John eventually got back to him. He immediately made amends.

> ***John:***   "Abby, that was a fantastic job you did getting all that backing. Do you need anything else for the project? You really came up with a great idea this time. Congratulations!"

This was a good "Why don't you speak for yourself, John?" lesson. Utilize person-to-person contact, eliminating the middleman, for important personal messages and you'll uplift the spirits of your subordinates.

Recognize a job well done

Praise, encouragement, reward, and incentives—all are vital to expressing appreciation and uplifting morale. You may be delighted to watch your workers develop, but that's not enough. Your *objective* is to let them know about your pleasure. You can't take anyone for granted. Even long-time loyal workers want recognition. Don't overlook praising them, too.

> **TIP:**   Patting the back knocks a chip off the shoulder.

Strategy   Pay attention to each and every one—with no exceptions.

Lanny, a 14-year veteran with the company, knows exactly what to do to ensure a smooth flow of material. Because he's so dependable, Brenda, the office manager, left him alone and didn't comment on his work.

Lanny misinterpreted Brenda's silence. He worried that he might be doing something wrong and they weren't telling him. Maybe he was going to be fired—after all the years he gave to the company! Lanny built up a head of steam, plotting destructive ways to get attention so that Brenda would have to ask him to straighten things out. Then she'd see how valuable he really was!

A childish reaction? Yes, but it was only because Lanny confided his fears to a mutual friend that Brenda became aware of the situation.

What to say   She set out immediately to reassure Lanny.

> ***Brenda:***   "Lanny, I don't know where this office would be without you. You are my most dependable worker. I know that sometimes I may seem to take your good work for granted, but really, I do appreciate all you do..."

Don't assume your workers know what you're thinking. Everyone needs periodic feedback and, if it's deserved, a pat on the back.

Encourage the worker who wants to improve

Loyalty goes both ways. When you show your allegiance to employees by going to bat for them, helping them through difficult assignments or arranging for them to learn new skills, they are more apt to stay with you and the company. They feel needed if you give them a sense of accomplishment.

> **TIP:** Stress performance, not conformance. Give your workers the right kind of feedback. Praise all attempts, even those that don't hit the mark. Appreciate the effort and the worker will continue to try harder. Your *objective* is to help your subordinates develop and make better use of their individual existing and potential skills and talents.

Strategy

(1) Identify ways you can help them develop. Study their reports. Watch for deviations or trends which you can help them interpret.
(2) Discuss with them your suggestions for their improvement or advancement.

Ruth is a concerned and conscientious boss who is anxious to help those subordinates who really want to improve. I asked her what she thought each worker needed to enhance his or her performance, both as a member of her team and in their personal lives. After considerable thought, she mentioned several ideas.

What to say   These were the ideas she listed which she later discussed individually with her staff.

"Marty needs additional training."

"A leadership course would help Byron."

"Barbara should improve her telephone skills."

"Written reports would force Angelia to think through problems."

"Joey would benefit most by representing the department."

The good leader improves morale by creating for subordinates opportunities for growth. In deciding on additional training, consider public speaking workshops or courses although you may have a problem keeping them down in their desks after they've seen the stage.

Express a True Desire to Consider Their Thinking

One of the best motivators is the message that you need your subordinates' suggestions to help you (and those above you) decide. You get them to tell you their ideas by instilling in your workers a sense of belonging, providing a way for them to give you the information, and then rewarding them for trying.

Discuss joint goals to instill a sense of belonging

The motivator talks about the end product. For a manufacturing company, it's flawless widgets; a law firm, properly represented clients; a social service agency, people receiving comprehensive care.

> **TIP:** Emphasize that it is the subordinate who makes it possible to achieve your end product, and in doing so everyone benefits. The objective is for subordinates to feel that the company or department is *their* company or department.

Strategy

> (1) Explain company goals telescopically, the big picture painted with wide strokes, and then zoom in microscopically to etch the details of the department.
>
> (2) Explain how your subordinates affect and are affected by the outcome.

Clay knew his people were turned off, but he didn't realize how abrasive it was every time he said, "C'mon, gang, I've got a goal to meet." Nobody was interested in his goal. They were interested in their own goals or how their goals related to the team effort.

What to say Clay changed his tune after I suggested that he change the "I" to "why" and add "we." Clay picked up the cue.

> **Clay:** "As we continue to expand, there are exciting things ahead for the company and for our department and for each of you. Specifically, we're going to be starting on..."

The efforts that brought results were not Clay's, but those of the whole team. To keep morale high, share the credit without hogging it all for yourself.

Explain your incentive system to your group

A written well-administered incentive plan says, in effect, that rewards aren't bestowed because the boss plays favorites. Anyone can earn the gold star. It pays to try your best.

The *objective* is to improve the service or product by reviewing with subordinates how one can climb the career ladder, and how this effort is reflected in increased salary and responsibility.

TIP: From paper copier to president, everyone wants to know what tangible benefits the company gives to reward their efforts. Spelling these out gives your staff confidence in your management.

Strategy Tell your whole team what's in it for them. Inform them how it pays, literally, for them to perform better.

Quint assumed everyone knew about the incentive system, but he learned differently after Lefty complained.

> *Lefty:* "Why should I try? What difference does it make if I knock myself out or just get by—it's all the same to the company."
>
> *Quint:* "That's not so, Lefty. We recognize extra effort and money-saving suggestions with incentive pay, days off, and educational and administrative leave. Our policy on giving raises, bonuses, and promotions is...Let's go over the manual together."

Having a plan isn't enough. You have to tell your staff about your plan and fully discuss it with them if your plan is to be an incentive to try harder.

Establish a system to elicit and exchange ideas

Dropping by worksites every few months for an occasional "What do you think?" is an impotent attempt at exchanging ideas. You need to establish a *system*, a mechanism for getting good participation and discussion. This might be a device for channeling suggestions from weekly staff meetings up to executive board meetings for consideration.

(1) *Meet Informally with Subordinates and Invite Them to Special Events.* Rotate workers, say six at a time, to an informal weekly Breakfast With The Boss, or to speak on an area of expertise at your board meeting. Invite workers to events that would be of special interest to them. For instance, Kelly's bookkeeper lit up upon hearing:

> **Kelly:** "Craig, the speaker at our trade association meeting will be talking about changes in tax regulations. Would you like to attend as my guest?"

(2) *Answer Your Own Phone.* You'll get suggestions, questions, and overall information from your subordinates that you might not otherwise hear. They'll be surprised and happy to get to talk directly to the boss.

(3) *Hold Your Calls for Your Staff.* It's disturbing and your subordinates perceive it as rude to be constantly interrupted when they're trying to make a point to you or follow a line of thinking. By holding the calls, you make them feel important—which they are. This kind of consideration breeds loyalty, and loyalty snuffs out sabotage. Before you start a meeting or an important discussion with a subordinate, tell your secretary,

> "Unless it's the big boss himself, I want no interruptions."

(4) *Call Instead of Writing Whenever Possible.* Don't wait to find the extra time to write notes to staff. The quicker, more personal telephone call keeps the lines open.

> "Phil, just wanted to let you know that I thought your suggestion was so good I'm sending it to the front office."

(5) *Use the Memo Appropriately.* Send a memo to keep your people informed of latest developments in the company, to interpret patterns and trends you see emerging that might affect their jobs, and to correct false rumors by presenting the facts, if only:

> "This is what we know at this point. Stay tuned."

Or you may have to give them some immediate reason for your turning to them for help, such as

> "Our costs have risen 23 percent in two years. To keep our heads above water, we need to make some changes..."

(6) *Use the Company Newsletter.* Start a readers exchange to bring suggested improvements from workers out in the field to

the upper echelon who are glued to their desks. Write a poignant, piercing, or provocative editorial. Answer questions employees have been asking, such as providing details on final pay raise negotiations and benefit changes.

(7) *Get Answers from Surveys.* Questionnaires, interviews, and surveys are a good way to gauge employee attitudes. When you sense a morale problem, tell them:

> "We're asking you to fill out and return this unsigned questionnaire. . .This gives you the freedom to be frank, even unkind, and your answers will also be more useful."

Whatever it is you decide to do, having a system for exchanging ideas is even more important than the ideas you exchange. When you express a true desire to consider the thinking of your subordinates, you elevate their spirits. And when you combine this with expressing your concern for them and your appreciation for their efforts, you automatically raise the morale of demoralized workers.

CHAPTER 13

⬭

Activating Nonperformers to Action

Among your subordinates you may find some who can't do the job, or who try to get out of it, and some who can't get going. How well are you communicating with these types? Choose your closest answer to the following questions. The interpretation of your choices follows.

1. After a few months, a new worker still is performing poorly. You

    (a) tell her she must go, without questioning the worker.
    (b) increase spoon-feeding, hoping she'll soon catch on.
    (c) review the work with her, but stress that learning is her responsibility.

2. When a veteran worker does poorly on a new job, you

    (a) say you feel bad, but it's his own fault that he's failing.
    (b) say you'll cover for him so he can meet his obligations.
    (c) offer him help to improve or suggest a transfer.

3. A good worker becomes chronically late with reports. You

    (a) warn her to stop trying to get out of her work.
    (b) suffer her poor performance since she's hard to replace.
    (c) gently probe for the real reason.

4. Despite warnings about taking two-hour lunches and busy-day absences, a worker continues his old ways. You

    (a) give him a sterner warning to shape up.
    (b) tolerate him because you've no one to replace him.
    (c) dismiss him for cause, even without a replacement.

5. Because too much clowning around keeps the staff from getting enough accomplished, you

    (a) initiate and enforce rules to prohibit office socializing.
    (b) lecture your group about meeting objectives.
    (c) renegotiate workloads insisting your staff finish the work.

6. A subordinate always begs for more time to perfect her work. You

    (a) demand she turn in whatever she has finished.
    (b) keep granting her more extensions.
    (c) you ask for a rough draft promising her more time later.

7. A worker keeps promising more than he knows he can deliver, making you miss your own deadlines. You

    (a) tell someone else to complete his assignments.
    (b) fall for another of his stalling tactics.
    (c) assign a partner to help him complete the work and plan more realistically.

8. A staff member does everything except the really important things you need. Because "lack of time" is just an excuse, you

    (a) warn her to get on the ball or else.
    (b) explain the importance of the data.
    (c) have a quiet talk to learn what's troubling her.

9. A subordinate wastes time by polishing minor jobs that should be left rough. You inform him

   (a) any one can see he's wasting time on the unimportant.
   (b) that he is to submit a time log every week.
   (c) of your specific priorities and allotted times.

10. You hired a worker because she's creative but also expect her to finish routine work which she's not doing. You

    (a) discuss the need to obey rules and procedures.
    (b) tell her you realize creative people need more time, so you'll take care of the routine.
    (c) ask an efficient, organized worker to team up with her.

Interpretation

If most of your answers are a's, you take a tough line. Your consistency is good, but you're not resolving the difficulty by saying anything to change poor behavior or work habits.

If most of your answers are b's, you are overly optimistic. You delude yourself into thinking everything will get better, but it won't until you intercede to make it better.

If most of your answers are c's, you are realistic and practical. You look for the reason behind the behavior and announce whatever is needed to bring about changes.

HOW TO CONVINCE POOR PERFORMERS TO GET GOING

Some people you supervise complicate your life and keep you from making it to the top. Ineffective and indifferent subordinates don't pull their part of the load, or don't do what they're supposed to, and you're held responsible. Whether they are poor workers or just work poorly in your turf, you need to treat them carefully so that you, as well as they, can survive. In this chapter, we'll discuss what you can say to move poor performers, nonperformers, and late performers. They fall into these general categories:

- Duds—they can't get going
- Deadbeats—they won't get going
- Procrastinators—who will get going later

Talking with Duds Who Can't Get Going

New workers, naturally, need your help. They may not know the routine and you have to stay with them until they can hold their own on the floor. Still, your leading subordinates through each step should be a short term involvement because it's their responsibility to learn. After you've clarified, demonstrated, given examples and suggestions and workers continue having trouble, chances are they either (1) have some personal problem they can't resolve (ask if you can help because this could be only a temporary setback) or (2) they are in the wrong job.

Winning the trust of your workers

Sometimes you "inherit" subordinates you don't want. Your boss, for example, asks you to accept workers from another department promising if they don't work out some other arrangement will be made. Had you been free to choose, you'd fill the vacancies with people having the specific skills you need. Now you have to train and hope for the best. If the "transfer" doesn't work out, you're trapped. You can't let your office suffer from inferior performance and you can't risk angry or hurt feelings asking the worker to leave. Your subordinate senses your annoyance and makes nervous mistakes.

> **TIP:** If you can't help poor workers improve, get them to leave happy *on their own volition*. Your objective is to find a different, more mutually satisfactory alternative and thereby escape between the horns of your dilemma.

Strategy Give the worker a fair chance, recognizing it's hard for both of you. Be his friend and he'll trust you. If you tell him you'll help him find another job he's better suited for, he'll listen to you.

When his advertising position was abolished during a reorganization move, popular old-timer Archy was transferred to Marketing where, despite receiving careful explanations, he wasn't doing too well. Bennett, his boss, was so impatient that every time he talked about Archy, he saw red. I told Bennett to throw down his cape and get out of the arena. This was no bullfight, but he had to take the dilemma by the horns and either help Archy improve or get him to leave.

What to say   Instead of again harping on what he expected, Bennett tried a complete reversal. He gave Archy the chance to talk about the situation.

> **Bennett:** "Archy, what seems to be the trouble? There must be a good reason why you're taking twice the time we anticipated."
>
> **Archy:** "Let me tell you about the red tape I've had to go through here..."
>
> **Bennett:** "Archy, I believe in your capabilities and I'd be happy to help you."

Bennett stayed behind him and finally won Archy's trust. But even with extra assistance, Archy continued to bungle.

> **Bennett:** "Archy, you're not making it here, however you have such a great way with words, you'd be a natural in sales. How about my making an appointment for you to see about transferring over there?"

Because Archy believed that Bennett was acting as a friend as well as a boss, he took his advice. Bennett solved the problem for both of them by helping Archy find his niche.

Admitting when workers are misplaced

There are times you find you've moved your subordinates up to a level of incompetence (the Peter Principle) or to a new job that doesn't utilize the skill and knowledge they previously enjoyed using. The job and the worker just don't match.

> **TIP:** Let these subordinates save face by admitting they were misplaced. Your *objective* is to get them productive again.

Strategy   Tactfully relieve mismatched workers from their current appointments and reassign them to something you know they can handle.

Angie was fretting that although Van had been dynamite in the field, he was turning out to be a dud in the office responsible for training other field workers. She worried if she switched him back to his former position, she would demoralize a fine worker. Not likely. Van was *already* demoralized. He saw he wasn't cut out to conduct training but he felt stuck.

What to say Tell the workers they are needed in other jobs—ones you know they can do well.

> **Angie:** "You know, Van, being training coordinator doesn't allow you to use your true talents and we can't find anyone to replace you in the field. I really need you back there."

If you acknowledge the worker's strong points, he can accept the change feeling puffed up and proud instead of crushed that he didn't make the grade.

Probing for reasons behind chronic problems

Another supervisory concern centers on subordinates who used to be punctual but now are chronically late. The excuses are limited only by their imaginations. Out of frustration, you are tempted to threaten them.

> **TIP:** Gently probe for the cause instead of berating the subordinate. The new behavior pattern is out of character. Your *objective* is to restore the workers to their previous level of satisfactory work performance.

Strategy Get the worker himself to identify and verbalize the real reason for the difficulty.

Brent complained that in the last three or four weeks, Conrad always had another excuse for his tardiness. The bridge got stuck in an up-position. His mother-in-law became ill. The power went off during the night and his alarm clock didn't ring until 8:00 A.M.

What to say I suggested that Brent sit him down and gently question him. Finally, Conrad mentioned his difficulty.

> **Brent:** "What do you think really causes you to be late?"

Conrad: "I don't know. No matter how hard I try, I can't make it. . .For the past month, we've had only one car in the family, and I've had to take my son to school, then drop my wife off at her job before I get here."

There it was, something tangible they could work on. Brent was able to adjust Conrad's working hours around his son's school hours. Together they worked out a plan (Conrad would cut his lunch hour in half) that allowed him to cope with the additional pressure. Nothing does any good until you can get the tardy worker to identify and verbalize the real reason.

Making mistakes sound easy to correct

To improve the quality of work turned in to you, first be sure your subordinates have whatever they need to do the job—equipment, tools, supplies, better ventilation, lighting, and noise control. After that, a good way to upgrade the work is simply to reject it by minimizing the amount of effort needed to correct it.

TIP: To help your subordinates achieve their potential, treat them as if they already can do whatever you want done. Your *objective* is to encourage your workers to improve, so make it sound uncomplicated.

Strategy Convey the challenge—convincing them that you're sure they'll do better. By telling them clearly and concisely what you want accomplished and how they can move from here to there, you make the inept action appear easy to rectify.

Lauren kept returning work to some subordinates whose efforts were a little below the standard she had set. Only minor changes were needed but, without receiving articulate and constructive feedback, the workers were upset thinking that everything had to be redone from scratch.

What to say Lauren needed to compliment them on what was done well and to point out clearly that what had to be altered could be easily accomplished.

> *Lauren:*   "Ralph, this is generally well prepared. However, there are a few minor mistakes I've checked. I'm sure you'll want to correct them to bring this piece up to your usual standard."

To increase the quality of performance, make the subordinate feel that what you want improved is something they can do easily.

Talking with Deadbeats Who Won't Get Going

Deadbeats shirk the work. You find yourself pleading with prima donnas or seeking some sorcerer's spell that will make them pitch in and do their share. Sometimes you run up against the attitude that all work and no play is interfering with their social life. When you've tried to motivate and there's still no improvement, give the problem back to the deadbeats explaining the consequences if they continue doing/not doing whatever is objectionable. If they persist, follow through on the promised reprimand.

Controlling the unreliable who want to skip out

You've met people who try to get away with anything they can. Give them an inch and they'll take a foot and eventually the whole yard. They will feign illness on your busiest day and never run out of excuses for not working. It can be frustrating when you know firing them will be a long, involved process.

TIP: Tell the deadbeats that closing their eyes to their responsibility fools no one. With their brand of blind man's bluff, they're tagged as unreliable. One more tag and they're out.

Strategy   The objective is to get the loafers to do what they're being paid for. Hold their feet to the fire with a firm, polite statement of policy: Produce or be replaced.

Lionel confided to me that Renee has been getting away with a lot lately, telling one lie after another to get out of her work. Last week, after Lionel carefully explained the conditions, Renee accepted a special assignment. But now she is not staying the required and agreed-to extra half-hour each day to get the work done.

What to say   Inform shirkers that you expect them to live up to their agreements.

> **Lionel:**   "Renee, if you had a legitimate excuse, like a broken leg, everyone would understand. But you are playing games and just skipping out on a promise. That's jumping a giant step backwards. Consider this a warning. Next time I'll take action."

When the deadbeats take advantage of you, and your positive reinforcement doesn't work, a no-nonsense warning often straightens them out.

Restraining pleasure seekers who convert the office to a social society

You try to keep your office running on an even keel. You divide dull, routine tasks so that no one is shackled with all of them. But sometimes subordinates are so busy trying to turn the office staff into a social society that even the challenging work doesn't get done. If workers have time for socializing on the job, either they are not being given enough to do or you are not enforcing definite deadlines, and the specific dates for completing each phase of a project.

> **TIP:**   Review your management style. Maybe you are not being strict enough. Or maybe you're being a little too stiff. After all, every red-blooded American likes to whoop it up a little.

Strategy   The *objective* is to regulate the amount of work so that your subordinates are always kept busy but are not constantly panting trying to catch up. The tactic is to reinforce your rules while providing for sufficient periods of informality.

George supervised a few people who got restless when they had to stay put to finish their jobs instead of getting together or leaving early for late afternoon partying. He decided to reduce the tension by easing up on his formality, planning for the whole group to lunch together or to have an after-hours party once in a while. This improved the atmosphere, but a few continued socializing on the job.

What to say   Tell them sternly that there's no room for employees who won't adhere to office policy.

> **George:**   "I want you to clearly understand that administrative orders forbid us to have parties here in the office. That's grounds for dismissal. I will no longer tolerate such acts of disobedience."

When balance and reasonableness don't work, the company won't miss one little, two little, three little convivialists. As it turned out, George never had to mention it again.

How to discuss stalling with the disinterested

An extra-curricular activity can cause you difficulty if the one you ask to do it keeps stalling you. Be careful or you may end up having to do the task yourself.

> **TIP:**   Those who stall at the start from lack of time or interest seldom shift into high gear. They have no spark to make them plug away.

Strategy   Your *objective* is simply to get the job done. The strategy is to put your foot down on a deadline and, if it's not done by then, immediately get a replacement. Don't allow anyone to play games.

Because Jon is quite talented, Frances asked him to take on an extra assignment, arranging the office exhibit at the college work fair. Jon said he'd let her know in a couple of days. He didn't. When Frances called back, Jon again wanted more time to reach a decision. Frances is wondering if Jon wants to be begged, or if she should look for someone else. The stalling stopped Frances in her tracks.

What to say   I suggested that Frances stop spinning her wheels and, in a friendly tone, stick to the original deadline. Had Jon been low on confidence, Frances's reassurance would have been sufficient. It was clear he wasn't interested.

> ***Frances:***   "Jon, I really need your answer now. Please level with me. Would you prefer that I find someone else?"

Jon was relieved that Frances let him off the hook. Recognize the stall as a disguised rejection and get someone else for the task.

Talking with Procrastinators Who Will Get Going Later

Each of us, from time to time, puts off something we don't feel like doing. However, procrastinators are different. Some are rebels, who try to get back at you for telling them what to do by not doing it. Some are afraid they'll fail, so they don't try.

Persuading perfectionists to turn in work

Some people suffer from paralysis of perfection. They set standards for themselves that are impossible to maintain. They are so afraid of preparing something that might have a flaw in it that it's hard to get them to turn in anything at all.

TIP: Reassure the perfectionists that they will have time later on to polish whatever product they turn in now.

Strategy   Reduce the pressure these workers put upon themselves. Your *objective* is to gain their cooperation.

Carlos was just berated by the boss for not having the planning survey. Carlos had entrusted the survey to his planner, Evan, who is a perfectionist. Evan rationalizes that if he doesn't give Carlos any work to examine, Carlos can't tell that it doesn't come up to the planner's extravagant expectations. So he delays and delays, hoping the problem will go away.

What to say   Carlos had to tell Evan there would be time in the future to hone his masterpiece.

> ***Evan:***   "I'm sorry, Carlos, but I have to have another week or two."

Carlos: "Evan, at this point, we just need a rough draft. You can have it back with plenty of time to prepare the final copy. I understand your rough draft falls short of what you want the finished survey to be, but having the draft now will really help us move the project along. I must have it now."

Generally, it's a good idea to encourage procrastinators to start with the easiest part just to get them going.

Bolstering good workers who feel insecure

The best controlled and self-assured people will, at times, put off a task for fear they aren't capable of doing it right. However some workers are so insecure that they delay taking action on excellent opportunities suited to their talents. If they wait long enough, the opportunities will fall through, and they can blame the loss on their being late rather than on their inadequacy.

TIP: The objective is to bolster the efficient worker who suddenly procrastinates. When you suspect the procrastination is due to unwarranted insecurity, help that subordinate identify the real reason for being unable to act.

Strategy   Gently probe by getting the subordinate to discuss the delaying tactics.

Department head Sandy was considering three people for the post of division director. She requested a summary proposal from each of them. Two turned in theirs, but Ellie gave a flimsy excuse. Sandy considered Ellie her best bet, an ambitious efficiency expert who had been handling her one-woman domain superbly. Was Ellie deliberately taking herself out of the competition? Was she telling herself that if she didn't get the promotion it was because she was late with the proposal? Obviously something was making Ellie procrastinate.

What to say   How could Sandy get Ellie to discuss her stalling? Without trying to push her, Sandy had to buoy up Ellie and help her become candid.

Sandy:	"Ellie, even the best jobs have some drawbacks. Could we talk about how you see the division director's position?"
Ellie:	"Boss, I've always accomplished everything I set out to do because efficient planning comes naturally to me. But I've always worked alone. I'm at a loss to know if I'd be able to get the cooperation I'd need as a division director."
Sandy:	"I can understand your concern and I think I can give you some very helpful advice on leading a group. Besides, I've watched you work closely with others and..."

With bolstering from Sandy, Ellie submitted the proposal under the deadline. Since she had a keen understanding of what had to be accomplished and the best plan for getting results, Ellie got the promotion. Now and then the procrastinator just needs a little reassurance.

Finding out why the rebels are angry

Why are some workers late with their work when they apparently have more than enough time for everything else—all nonessential tasks?

TIP: When a worker claims a shortage of time and this is obviously an excuse for procrastinating, try questions instead of sarcasm or threats. Your objective is to find out what's really causing the delay.

Strategy Provide a calm, nonthreatening atmosphere and interrogate in a friendly manner.

Adam almost threw a monkey wrench into the deal when he was late with the background data. His boss, Theo, stormed at him, asking why he would procrastinate knowing how important the data was. Adam claimed he didn't have enough time which Theo knew was not the case.

What to say Theo saw his accusations weren't getting anywhere. He reversed his tactics and began again, friend to friend.

> **Theo:** "Look, Adam, maybe my time estimation was wrong; and if so, I'm sorry. But you seem angry about something. I'd really like you to tell me what's the matter."
>
> **Adam:** "You want to know, let me tell you about this crummy operation. I work my tail off and..."

Adam needed someone compassionate enough to absorb his anger and turn him around so that he could get back to work. At times the procrastinator's delay is a veiled attempt to get your attention.

Subduing workers who make minor chores into major productions

These are workers who give you an earful or an eyeful on every trifle, then fret they haven't time for many important tasks. No wonder. Every minor chore becomes a whopping production when they get into the act.

TIP: First make sure your standards for minor tasks are realistic. You don't want to impose extra work over the mundane and unimportant.

Strategy Your objective is to maintain a high standard when standards count. Help the magnifier understand how to apportion time and energy.

Warde complained that Flora gives each job her grand design. She hasn't grown up emotionally. He's tried telling her that some jobs require one's best efforts and some don't, but it was like talking to a child.

What to say At this point Warde had to make her understand the difference between tasks that are very important and those that just need a lick and a promise.

> **Warde:** "Flora, you have a mature mind that can make this distinction. To dwell on the insignificant makes it swell out of proportion. Frankly, it's a

skimpy accomplishment scarcely worth your time and certainly not worthy of self-esteem. From now on, I am going to mark the less important papers 'quickly' and expect you to process them as fast as you can."

He added a deadline date to every assignment he gave Flora. The system worked well for Warde.

How to encourage creative workers burdened by routine

Creative people can be difficult to supervise because, by nature, they see different ways to do things. Quick, original, and adaptive, they may not want to conform to your rules and may not produce to your time table.

TIP: Recognize when creative workers need extra latitude to be productive. Your objective is to try to protect them from administrative impatience.

Strategy Find a way to unshackle creative subordinates from some of the routine in order to give them more thinking time.

Wyler's task was to come with unusual ways to present old ideas. Raymond tried to be non-judgmental with Wyler to give him breathing room until he could get going. When Wyler wanted to wear his "lucky tennis hat" all day in the office since he couldn't get any ideas to jell without it, Raymond gave in to his idiosyncrasy. Even with the hat, Wyler kept missing due dates. He claimed he was bogged down in paperwork.

What to say Although tempted, Raymond didn't assume Wyler's obligation. Wyler was still responsible for carrying out the assignment, but Raymond did come up with needed help to get him going.

Raymond: "Wyler, I've asked Judy to work with you on the project. Her organized mind will plow through the pesky details that may be worrying you. And talking over the project with a partner should help you spark some new thoughts."

The very act of explaining one's ideas to a partner can unblock the creative mind.

* * *

When the work isn't being done or isn't being done right, ask yourself if you have duds, deadbeats, or procrastinators. Look for the reason behind the behavior so that you can influence your subordinates to change poor behavior into productive performance.

CHAPTER 14

Encouraging Troublesome Workers to Act Responsibly

Any group may have a few who never grew up. They mean to follow through, yet never do. If you're grumbling about lazy workers, and you're tired of nagging, try to learn why they're dragging behind. Perhaps the fault is in your leadership technique. Take a closer look at yourself. Here are some questions to help you decide if you are encouraging or discouraging the responsible behavior of your subordinates.

1. In making assignments,

    (a) do you hook anyone you can?
    (b) budget your workers to match their experience, skill, time, and interest with the specific jobs?

2. When coaching your subordinates,

    (a) do you teach by telepathy?
    (b) transfer your thoughts to a written reference of rules and reasons?

3. As for explaining the importance of even routine tasks,

    (a) are you a taciturn trainer, keeping your thoughts to yourself?

    (b) do you tell each worker what's expected (why, when, where, how) and how that job figures into the total effort?

4. In motivating workers,

    (a) are you an initiative killer, stifling all opinions?

    (b) do you draw out their solutions rather than solving their problems before they know they have any?

5. If placing blame is an issue,

    (a) are you a buck-passer, refusing to acknowledge and apologize for your mistakes or those of your staff?

    (b) do you shoulder responsibility when someone under you errs, quietly correcting the boner?

6. When it comes to building confidence among your staff,

    (a) are you an ego destroyer, insensitive to their needs?

    (b) do you encourage publicly and privately, willing to praise an idea not your own?

7. As for accessibility to your subordinates,

    (a) are you hard to find, playing catch-me-if-you-can?

    (b) is it usually easy to get in touch with you to discuss a problem?

8. During emergencies or near-emergencies,

    (a) are you likely to push the panic button?

    (b) do you, for instance, find a substitute if a worker must stay home until Junior is over the mumps?

9. You keep your unit operating at a

    (a) hurried, anxiety-ridden, rush-rush-rush pace.

    (b) flexible pace, easing up when everyone is tired.

10. The manner in which you yourself obey regulations says you

    (a) consider yourself above the rules.

    (b) respect the system and the chain of command.

11. When it comes to setting standards,

(a) it's clear that for you, anything goes.

(b) you set high standards, tactfully rejecting inferior work and helping the worker improve.

If you didn't get all b's, you may need to revamp your approach. Make certain you've explained to each one the relevance of the job to the total effort, given each person some say in the decisions affecting his or her work, and told each one precisely what you want done.

HOW TO MAKE DIFFICULT WORKERS MORE ACCOUNTABLE

Most workers are self-disciplined, self-motivated, pleasant, and productive. But some others, to put it delicately, are difficult. Beware what you say to the assorted assailers and wailers who are under your supervision for they can trip you on your way up. Here are some guidelines for talking to, and hopefully improving the behavior of, subordinates best described as:

- Sharpshooters
- Snitches
- Whiners

Guidelines for Dealing with Camouflaged Attacks on Your Authority

Because they feel unappreciated and want to get your attention, your assistants may attack you under the guise of doing something else. Prevention is the easiest route. To discourage being riddled by sharpshooters, first make sure subordinates feel free to discuss any problem with you, both privately and at staff meetings. If you are still the target of veiled verbal shots, here are various ways to expose the culprits and get them to behave.

When barbs are disguised as jokes

Your sense of humor is as good as anyone else's and you can certainly go along with a joke. But when the remarks are obviously intended to make you, the boss, appear ridiculous in front of your staff, that's no laughing matter.

TIP: Be sure to recognize accomplishments of subordinates not only to avoid their darts, but also because these people are vital to your attaining your goals. Your objective is to restore respect and reduce abuse.

Strategy   For the next attack

(1) Take the offense (being careful not to get defensive).

(2) Smoke out the sniper by asking a few questions. Get the sniper out in the open where you can expose the antics.

Ken thought once he got to be a division director, he'd be safe from snipers, certainly among his own crew. He didn't count on their attacks cloaked as humor or their manipulations that could erode his authority. For instance, in advance of a staff meeting, Ken distributed a report to set the stage for an informed discussion on the strategy being proposed. Up popped Bentley.

Bentley:	"Boss, you're the best thing for my insomnia. I read this last night and it put me right to sleep."

Bentley laughed, as though it were a joke. One more in a long list of barbs he kept zinging at Ken. The others sat there, uncomfortable, not knowing whether to laugh or be still. If Ken came down on Bentley, he'd appear to have no sense of humor. But he had to regain control.

What to say   Use a light bantering tone and wear a grin to confront this type of joker.

Ken:	"Bentley, are you saying my report is dull?"
Bentley:	"Boss, it takes ten cups of coffee to get through it. Ha, ha."
Ken:	"Bentley, are you making fun of me? Did anyone else have difficulty reading the report?" (still in a light tone) "Why not point out to us the specific places that drag."
Bentley:	"Well...uh...nothing really in particular...It was just a joke, boss."

Ken: (still casual and smiling) "Okay, then, let's move on to legitimate reactions to the report and how we can improve it."

Poised and friendly, you can regain control of the discussion and force the jokers to limit the remarks to constructive suggestions.

When they get results by bending the rules

If you don't stop subordinates who achieve results by breaking rules, you find yourself courting their influence and under their power.

TIP: When you're being intimidated by subordinates who force you to kowtow, call their bluff. Let them huff and puff. They can't blow your department down.

Strategy Re-establish your rules and stick to them. The *objective* is to have your whole team pulling together as one entity. This won't work if you allow even one subordinate to twist or disobey your regulations, whatever the reason.

Aggressive Della runs roughshod over everyone including Andy, her boss. Rules and precedent mean nothing to her. She does everything her own way ignoring his directives. The trouble is, she gets results. So Andy finds himself afraid to antagonize her lest he lose the benefits she produces from having good connections. Nevertheless, giving in to Della's threats such as "Where would this office be without me?" is costing Andy his self respect. And maybe his future.

What to Say Andy had to hold his ground, uniformly expecting everyone to adhere to the rules.

Della: "Andy, I won't have this week's account sheets until next Monday because I've got a sweet deal I'm working on to get us. . ."

Andy: "Della, the account sheets have to be turned in by Thursday or it throws everything else off schedule. That's the rule, and I expect you and everyone else to abide by it."

Getting impressive results through an intimidator's favors drains your spirit and discourages your staff. So speak up and temporarily settle for less. When your whole department starts working together, you'll soon have a stronger and better team.

Handling workers who are determined to rule or ruin

You have a couple of smart, capable workers who are difficult to supervise because they're overzealous in ramming through their pet projects. They seem determined to destroy anything (or anyone) in their way.

TIP: Your objective is to maintain and control your unit. Get your excessively aggressive subordinates to be part of the team. Calmly enlighten them without lighting their way in a charged atmosphere because one accusatory spark could cause an explosion.

Strategy Use peer pressure—a source of support you may have overlooked—to bring the aggressors back into line.

Laurie, a fair-minded executive, finds Dan's nagging so persistent until, in desperation, she gives in to her subordinate rather than insulting him. We decided that Laurie would call a special meeting to discuss only one item, how to improve participation at the staff meetings. Without ever pointing a finger, she nailed down the problem.

Laurie:	"I learned that some of you don't feel you can talk freely at our meetings. . .that when you voice an opinion, it gets chopped into little pieces."
Dan:	"There sure are some thin skins around here."

Laurie stuck to the basic rules of debate (discussed in the next chapter) and let Dan, too, have his say. The others joined in exerting group pressure on Dan to behave. While an open discussion lets a group enjoy the bright rays of progress, it also lets a bossy worker adjust to the glare.

Diluting the strength of troublesome cliques

When you find yourself facing a clique among your subordinates, your first reaction is to ponder how to muzzle the musketeers. Generally, it's safer to avoid a frontal attack upon a clique, a move which could possibly split your office into enemy camps.

> **TIP:** If a clique simply bolsters those who are weak by themselves, it probably meets their need and doesn't impede. Those who cling to each other for support are no threat—leave them alone. Your concern is with the power-hungry, and the objective is to maintain control not letting a few subordinates gang up, making decisions you should be making.

Strategy Separate from each other clique members whose decisions are based on wielding power. Tempt each one individually and subtly by assigning them to different tasks, ones that blend with specific, natural interests. If possible, place them in different locations.

Gretchen would like to break up Mabel, Margo, and Olive who compose a clique that works as a block. If one wants to do something, they all do and this results in a power play.

What to say Gretchen decided to move them in three different directions where they'd no longer be working closely together everyday. She made the new assignments without referring to the clique.

When you sense your authority is being undermined, don't clobber the clique. Dissolve it or dilute its potential power by separating the members.

Guidelines for Dealing with Snitches and Other Unasked-for Helpers

These subordinates operate under the pretext of assisting you, but they really aim to exert influence over you.

What to say when they leap in
without authorization

Some subordinates are determined to manipulate you by making you feel grateful to them. They appear most anxious to be helpful and given the slightest opportunity, they leap in. But they're in over their heads when they leap before looking for authorization.

TIP: Turn down help offered by subordinates who ignore regulations, snatch up bargains that are cheaper by the dozen and create gross bedlam. Your *objective* is to keep control and have everyone play by the same rules.

Strategy State very clearly that all acts must be authorized and spell out the consequences for unauthorized acts.

Carmen committed the agency to send a speaker without first checking to see who was available. Too embarrassed to cancel, Bea, her director, finally found someone to give the talk. Carmen also bought exotic plants for each desk because she could get them wholesale. They could not be returned. Bea signed the petty cash voucher, feeling trapped.

What to say In the process of explaining her frustration to me, Bea realized that Carmen was being devious. From then on she got her to tow the mark.

> **Bea:** "Carmen, I know you mean well, but you've placed us in an awkward position. If every employee committed the agency without approval, we'd be out of business. The next time *you* will cancel unauthorized appointments, and the cost of items you purchase without signed requisitions will be deducted from your salary. Your ideas are good, but I won't bail you out any more."

That was enough to convince Carmen to back off from her disguised manipulation—giving "help" in order to make herself appear more important. Be firm to stop such childish behavior.

What to say to regain control from one running the show

Your team needs guidance. In areas where you tend to nap, a competent assistant will close the gap, filling the vacuum that a lack of leadership creates. You have a choice: either swallow your pride and let your assistant lead the parade or step to the front of the line.

TIP: Put yourself in charge again. Admittedly, this is a little tricky after you've let the leadership slip away. However, you can achieve your objective—to regain control and still keep the valuable help your assistant offers.

Strategy Talk individually to each staff member, reviewing assignments and furnishing useful data.

Bryan's been with the company for years. He helps Len, his director, with practical ideas, follows through on whatever he tackles, and tactfully assists his peers. Len's afraid of losing the lead. Bryan is actually running the show. The staff go to Bryan, not Len, for advice.

What to say Len had a separate session with each subordinate. At the end of the individual meetings, Len reminded each one to call *him*.

> *Len:* "Whenever you have any ideas you want to discuss or any questions, don't hesitate to call on me."

Handled this way, a capable assistant could keep his fingers in all the pies while the boss could have his cake and eat it, too.

What to say to self-appointed informants

What can you do with information from a snitch, especially if the snitch is right? Ordinarily, when any two subordinates are having a problem working together, you let the two of them resolve it themselves. If the problem persists, you may find yourself in the middle and that's not a good place to be.

TIP: Don't let subordinates hide behind the cover of being (self-appointed) informants. Your objective is to get snitches to solve their own problems without resorting to tattling.

Strategy Throw the problem back to the subordinates. Make them own up to being behind the accusations.

Roz ladles out guilt. It may be our right to voice complaints, but Roz has perfected her performance to a steady, high-pitched sing-song. Point up a problem that needs attention and she makes it your fault that it occurred. More difficult for Dee is that Roz is an informer. She came into Dee's office to tattle on Charlie, her latest target, saying she was behind with the statements only because Charlie is always late in tabulating. Dee tried to get Roz to talk it over with Charlie.

Dee: "Have you tried to work this out with Charlie? Maybe you could go to lunch together?"

Roz: "Boss, it wouldn't do any good. Charlie never listens to me when I tell him what has to be done."

Dee: "Try again."

What to say Predictably, Roz came back with more news about Charlie.

Dee: "Well, Roz, how about my telling Charlie what you've said and give him a chance to. . ."

Roz: "No, Dee, that's not a good idea."

Dee: "Then suppose I set up a meeting to help you and Charlie work this out?"

Roz: "Ah, no, thank you."

Dee: "Well, Roz, when you want to get together with Charlie, give me a call."

The next move is now up to Roz. She knows if she comes to Dee again, her boss will make her come out of hiding and assume some of the responsibility for solving her own problem.

Guidelines for Dealing with Whiners

Among the garden varieties of malcontents are those who have to let you know how hard they work. Some are overly critical of their own efforts. Others are always down and manage to demoralize everyone else.

When martyrs say no one else does anything

Martyrs smother themselves in meetings and reports in order to fill a fathomless personal void or engulf an ever-present problem. They can't understand why you, too, don't live and breathe the organization. They may complain that no one else does anything, but they *enjoy* their overtime labor.

TIP: Tighten your control over martyrs. Politely refuse their offers of additional help when "no one else is doing it." Your *objective* is to prevent martyrs from running roughshod over their colleagues even if you can't save them from themselves.

Strategy Unsaddle the stubborn-as-a-mule workhorses and redistribute the burden.

Sally supervises a martyr, Nat, and is concerned on two counts. He makes everyone else feel tense and, if he continues his pace, he's probably heading for severe physical problems. Nat has no time for friends, only for frenzy. He schedules every minute, never adding a brief do-as-you-please period into his time budget. Sally has tried to slow Nat down by limiting him to a reasonable workload.

What to Say Finally, Sally sounded a warning that made Nat consider, temporarily, the reality of his compulsive behavior.

> *Sally:* "Nat, experts agree the healthy mind and body require relaxation. If you continue to go along from day to day, never having a time to call your own, you won't have any problems in your old age. You won't be around for that."

One warning won't change compulsive behavior, but you can insist that the martyrs do only their fair share of work to keep them from laying guilt on everyone else.

When naggers continually nag themselves

You don't always need two to tangle. Sometimes you see bickering in reverse. The nagger nags himself. Label these subordinates "self-pecked." They constantly complain that their own ideas aren't any good, or that their work is poor when actually they do quite well and regularly follow through. You would like to tell them to grow up, but you're too well mannered to be mean.

TIP: Refuse to pay emotional blackmail to the self-pecked. Give these constant complainers plenty of reassurance and then don't bite when they fish for additional compliments. Your *objective* is to teach them to replace self-depreciation with emotional maturity.

Strategy

(1) Keep giving these workers responsibilities you're certain they can handle. This is not a mathematical formula, but figure that insecurity diminishes in ratio to each little success.

(2) Stop giving in to their childish habits. Explain the potential loss to them from begging for compliments.

As her supervisor, Jamie found Winnie's belittling habit irksome. She continually put herself down instead of gracefully and rightfully accepting credit for her careful planning and implementing.

Winnie:	"My report was terrible, wasn't it, Jamie?"
Jamie:	"Winnie, on a scale of one to ten, I'd give it an eight."
Jamie:	"You coordinated an excellent orientation session, Winnie."
Winnie:	"Oh, most of that came from the plan in the manual."

What to say   Jamie had tried reassurance and Winnie persisted in begging for more. One day he asked Winnie to represent the office at the board meeting and he was prepared for her response:

> **Winnie:**   "Boss, are you sure you want me to represent the office?"
>
> **Jamie:**   "Winnie, I think you are capable of representing us. However, if that makes you uncomfortable, I can send Margaret instead."

At last, it sunk in. When Winnie realized that depreciating her efforts as a means of begging for compliments almost cost her a great opportunity, she stopped the self-pecking routine.

When wet blankets drown every idea before it's considered

Some subordinates forecast dark clouds about everything that comes up. Their icy downpour drenches any idea, discouraging everybody from even suggesting anything more.

TIP: Keep your own optimism under control as you strive to downplay the influence of cynics or alarmists. No one wants to sound like a cockeyed optimist going off half-cocked so, remember, your objective is reasonableness.

Strategy

   (1) Direct your group toward objective consideration of the matter.
   (2) Determine realistically if you have the right resources or experience to carry out the idea.

Arlie was trying to keep a high level of enthusiasm within his unit but he was having a tough time overcoming Scott's pessimism. It pervaded the room whenever a new idea was presented. Scott's gloomy predictions not only drowned out creative thinking, but was also downright depressing.

What to say   As the boss, it was up to Arlie to balance the discussion by seeking realism.

Scott: "It won't work. I know. We tried it before."

Arlie: "Scott, this idea sounds a little different to me. I think we might see how it compares to our past efforts. You know, we do have a serious delivery problem in that area that we are going to have to deal with..."

This type of leadership from Arlie encouraged the others to join in.

Encouraging workers who don't feel appreciated

Even good workers may put in poor performances when they're feeling blue. They may assume their jobs aren't essential because no one ever told them they are. Occasional compliments from the boss don't seem to help as long as subordinates think they're not making a contribution.

> **TIP:** Your objective is to give these workers a psychological boost. Try, for example, a name plate, a sign on the door, personalized business cards, or a change of title.

Strategy   Call the job something else. Change the *working* title to a more vital sounding one.

Sharon is in charge of operating the copiers. She saw no relationship between her job and the success of the company. To her, running the copiers wasn't exciting or challenging and certainly not important. Her supervisor Sonny told her how valuable she was and how once she promised to do something he could stop worrying about it. He also said that they'd probably have to close up shop without Sharon's services. But she was hard to convince.

What to say   I suggested to Sonny that he change her working title. He went a step further:

Sonny: "Sharon, I've had this sign printed for your desk. You are now our new duplication unit manager."

Whenever she looked at the sign, Sharon stopped thinking of herself as Clerk-Typist II, the Personnel Department listing. Changing her title helped change her attitude.

What to say to two quarreling workers

Good managers lead, and all major problems within their departments should be brought to them. The key word is major. You don't want to be caught in petty bickering, especially with endless phone calls.

TIP: Don't go another round next time the bell rings.

Strategy Lead with a right to the heart of the problem. Your objective is to let your people know that you won't allow squabbling to affect the work.

Heather's phone kept ringing with tales of petty, personal grievances among her staff. She was spending entirely too much trying to play mediator, and in doing so was encouraging the condition to persist.

What to say Heather finally saw the need to stop the pettiness. The next caller heard:

> **Heather:** "Tammy, this is something you and Monty had better straighten out privately and immediately. While your personal misunderstanding concerns only the two of you, our office can't function well unless we all work together. There just isn't room here for those who jeopardize the operation because they can't control their personal feelings."

Her people got the message. You needn't get caught up in subordinate bickering. Just strongly announce that you don't want that kind of behavior.

* * *

Since some subordinates are not what they seem to be, a supervisor has to grasp substance, not shadow. Assert your leadership and make your people act responsibly if they use humor, favors, bickering, and even self-depreciation to try to control you or the situation.

CHAPTER 15

$\Large\text{(}\quad\quad\quad\quad\text{)}$

Three Cardinal Rules
for Running
Dynamic Meetings

QUIZ #15. ARE YOU PREPARED TO PRESIDE?

Meetings should sharpen your leadership skills, develop your staff, and build group pride and enthusiasm. What would you say in each of the following situations? The interpretation of your choices follows.

1. Although you're no expert on parliamentary procedure, to get results when presiding at small staff meetings, you

   (a) strictly enforce parliamentary rules.
   (b) are flexible in adapting rules.
   (c) forget traditional procedures and talk as one of the gang.

2. To improve the quality of the ideas presented, you

   (a) distribute meeting agendas to all participants well in advance of meetings.
   (b) express your disappointment in the suggestions given.
   (c) invite outside speakers to each meeting.

3. Promoting your pet project, you introduce the project manager

    (a) by supplying background, and then you add interesting but not vital points that he leaves out.

    (b) without remarks, being careful not to reveal partiality.

    (c) by expressing your confidence, and not adding any points that he chooses to omit.

4. You spot squirms that say a subject's been exhausted. You

    (a) warn the group not to make repetitious comments.

    (b) call for a vote if appropriate, or go to the next item.

    (c) call on everyone who's not yet spoken.

5. Everyone is up-tight after you announce budget cuts. You

    (a) try a little humor to release some of the tension.

    (b) say, unfortunately, they have to bite the bullet.

    (c) tell them how painful this is to you, too.

6. You have strong convictions about an agenda item, so you

    (a) tell your staff your view before they start talking.

    (b) keep still, even after discussion, to remain impartial.

    (c) present your view after the staff discussion.

7. Since certain information has to be funneled to your staff, you call a meeting

    (a) to distribute copies to everyone.

    (b) to answer any questions needing your clarification.

    (c) because giving them new information promotes comraderie.

8. Your follow-up pattern to a good suggestion requiring your boss's permission is to

    (a) caution your group that approval is out of your control.

    (b) immediately submit an interoffice memo to see if you get a response.

    (c) bring the idea to your boss and report the response at the next meeting.

9. When a controversial issue comes up and you already have a headache, you

   (a) postpone the matter until the next meeting.
   (b) go around the room giving each one two minutes to comment.
   (c) use the blackboard to separate the pros and cons.

10. Your group's general suggestions are not dealing directly with the problem, so you

   (a) ask everybody to call out suggestions which you write on the blackboard.
   (b) follow with a few penetrating questions to get at the issue.
   (c) ask them to stick to the basic issue under discussion.

Interpretation

Group I: 1a, 2b, 3a, 4a, 5b, 6a, 7a, 8b, 9b, 10c
Group II: 1b, 2a, 3c, 4b, 5a, 6c, 7b, 8c, 9c, 10b
Group III: 1c, 2c, 3b, 4c, 5c, 6b, 7c, 8a, 9a, 10a

If most of your answers are in Group II, you tend to be rigid, proper, and look more at form or procedure than content. Some subordinates think they should salute when you enter the room. Sometimes your remarks are misinterpreted as lectures or scolding. Try to relax and enjoy the meetings more.

If most of your answers are in Group I, you tend to be imaginative, flexible, practical. Your eye's on the goal, you seek solutions, foresee consequences, and will take a risk to get out of a rut. Be careful about bending the rules too far.

If most of your answers are in Group III, you tend to be more interested in making and keeping friends than in leading your group. Sometimes you miss the mark because you don't want to offend anyone. Be aware that a misdirected sense of fair play might make you appear weak.

HOW TO GET THE RESULTS YOU WANT WHEN PRESIDING

Meetings are an indispensable part of office routine and you *can* make them exciting and profitable. Armed with good manners and common sense, there's no excuse to refuse to hold regularly scheduled meetings because you're afraid of parliamentary procedure or can't control group discussion. To remind you what to do before, during and after your meetings, you'll find a Meeting Checklist at the end of this chapter.

In Chapter 10, we discussed how participants could use meetings to showcase their abilities and win favorable notice. Now let's look at what the boss can say from the other side of the table to promote group pride, comraderie and enthusiasm. Whatever the meeting purpose—to exchange or clarify information, train workers, air or solve problems, decide or recommend policy or procedure, or get support for a company goal—you'll find that three tactics pay dividends and lead to more dynamic sessions.

- Keep the discussion moving
- Come across as flexible—avoid being rigid or frigid
- Reach decisions and accomplish the purpose—don't vacillate.

Keep the Discussion Moving

Getting everyone to talk and keeping the discussion gushing takes both prepared participants and a good presider. You politely stop some speakers and encourage others, jump in to clarify when the group is in the middle of a muddle, summarize at each step, and refrain from talking too much to give the others a chance. On your agenda, circle the points you want to emphasize and jot quips to toss off "spontaneously" between agenda items. Occasionally schedule audio-visuals, presentations, and guest speakers to break up the monotony.

Make sure your staff is prepared to report and discuss

Something should happen as a result of your meeting. Your staff is more informed, better trained, organized, or inspired. Results don't happen by themselves. You have to make it happen. The first step is preparing your people to participate by communicating the meeting purpose to them ahead of time. Your objective is to make the meeting well worth the cost of everyone's time.

> **TIP:** If you want your group to hear enthusiastic reports, you can't leave it to chance. Good short reports take time to prepare—to put facts in logical order, develop an attention-getting opener, a recommendation, or other closing.

Strategy

(1) Distribute the meeting agenda ahead of time, early enough for participants to check facts, make calls, or just think through an issue before spouting off.

(2) Review with each scheduled speaker the type and length of report to deliver.

Rona asked me how to pep up her meetings. Her chief complaint was that the meetings dragged. It was like a schoolroom show-and-tell time with such unprepared and uninspired accounts as Ginny's.

> "I don't have anything to report except we signed a contract with..."

What to say We worked out a quick phone format for Rona to use in advance of the meeting.

> ***Rona:*** "Ginny, please be prepared to report Friday on the progress with the Clayton contract, and to answer questions as to how this affects each of our units. We'll plan ten minutes in all. OK?"

A successful meeting starts long before you call it to order. You communicate your purpose to participants and when necessary, supply them data so that they can discuss agenda items; and you review with speakers the talks they'll be giving.

Discuss problems while they'll still small

A staff meeting is a fine forum for introducing techniques to cope with common problems. Your objective is to recognize when such help is needed in order to make it an agenda item.

> **TIP:** Hoist your antenna to catch signals of potential trouble. Watch for patterns emerging. Note if a few staff people are having the same difficulty. Then prepare participants to use the meeting to deal with symptoms before there's a crisis.

Strategy In advance of the meeting, distribute to your staff background information on the particular trouble spot.

Clay mentioned to me that Keith came by his desk.

Keith: "It's been a rough week, Clay. A client kept screaming at me over an error she had made. Must be the full moon. Angie told me her client threw a tray at her."

I asked Clay how they handled staff abuse, and he said they'd never really discussed it.

What to say We decided Clay would find and distribute copies of good articles on that topic prior to the next meeting. Having prepared his staff with background data, Clay was able to pull answers out of the group with questions such as:

Clay: "What steps might we take when a client gets abusive?"

When you begin to hear the same problem over and over, it may be time to schedule a discussion and get the benefit of group thinking.

How to start and stop talking on time

If a routine meeting goes past an hour, you've probably planned too many complex issues. A good rule is to call a time-out after 90 minutes because, by then, the attention span is shot. When you have guest speakers, shorten your agenda and advise them how long to talk. Stand up and walk next to guests who speak too long—they'll get your message. But remind your staff if they must leave before speakers are through, sit where they can't see them exit.

> **TIP:** As you preside, watch the time. Your *objective* is to complete the meeting in the specified time. It's your obligation not to keep participants longer than you promised.

Strategy

   (1) In planning the meeting, allocate *x*-number of minutes for each item and add this time schedule to the agenda you distribute.
   (2) Start at the designated time without waiting for latecomers. A formal meeting needs a quorum; an informal meeting doesn't.

Norman always started and stopped late, interfering with everybody's appointments. Doting on dawdlers, he punished the punctual who now were also beginning to arrive late. At most, I suggested, wait a ten-minute grace period, but it's better to begin as scheduled.

What to say   To institute a change, we worked out a stern message for Norman to deliver.

   Norman: "At the next meeting, the last one into the room has to clean out the coffee pot. The rest of us had three cups this morning waiting for you to show. No excuses. Next time we start at 9:30 sharp!"

By simply enforcing his own rules, Norman was able to start and stop on time.

How to encourage your staff to talk at meetings

If you find you have subordinates who wait until your meeting is over to question why an action was or wasn't taken, you have to wonder why they don't speak up at the meeting. How do you receive their comments or questions? Could it be that your reception to any suggestion is discouraging, argumentative, or fear-producing?

Here are a few reasons people give for not participating and what you might say to encourage the reluctant to join in.

Reason #1: "It will make me a moron if I ask. Everyone else seems to understand."

Encouragement: "Is the procedure clear? Does anyone want to discuss it some more?"

Reason #2: "I don't want to be alone on a limb. I'll wait to line up my supporters after the meeting."

Encouragement: "Thank you, Ann, that's a new slant we'll want to consider." Accept each idea graciously and politely. Even if you don't agree, don't argue. Stay impartial during the discussion.

Reason #3: "I don't understand their pompous ideas. They don't give anyone else a chance. If I can't join 'em, I'll lick 'em. I'll find flaws those smart guys have overlooked."

Encouragement: When it's always the same few who dominate discussion, say "Excuse me, Micky, let's hear from a few who haven't spoken yet."

Reason #4: "The last time I gave my opinion, they jumped all over me. They won't get my good ideas any more."

Encouragement: "Lois, I know you've had experience with that system. It would help us to know your evaluation of it." Fire a few direct questions to the timid or intimidated.

How to speak to inconsiderate talkers

If you don't control the discussion, others will. Among them are such inconsiderate talkers as:

(1) *Rude participants who talk to each other instead of to the group.* When you allow your subordinates to get away with this, the meeting is boring and you've lost control. Don't compete with distractions—that only makes more commotion. When the talkers start, stop the meeting. Smile silently. Break off in the middle of your own sentence or interrupt the speaker.

Speaker: "It seems logical to assume that if we—"

You: "Excuse me, Camille, not everyone can hear your interesting remarks. We'll wait a moment for silence before we continue."

(2) *People who devour meeting time.* Enforce your rules. These gluttons for attention can be stopped with

> "Liz, we appreciate the several good ideas you've given us. But since everyone hasn't had the chance to speak, let's save your other comments until later."

(3) *Elaborators who make good points, but prolong discussion.* Control them by establishing and sticking to a reasonable time frame; for example, no one speaks longer than three minutes at a time without group approval.

> "Alice, you're over the time limit. I'm sure you, too, want to hear what the others think about this."

(4) *Ramblers who go on and on, talking all around the point they're making.* Their thoughts are worth considering if you can turn them off when they come up for air.

> "That's an interesting idea, Linus. What specific action do you suggest we take?"

How to get the discussion back on the track— with tact

To return to the real issue under discussion, here are a few phrases to say to detractors.

Detractor	Sample Comment
Railroaders push for quick decisions without ample debate.	"Yes, time is passing, but I know you want everyone to have the chance to talk."
Divergers go off in tangents until everyone forgets the issue.	"I'm sure we'll want to explore that carefully, but right now the point is. . .Do you agree it'd be a good idea to. . ."

| Sore Losers are reluctant to give in after their ideas are refused overwhelmingly. | "It was important for us to hear all views. Thanks, Sy." |
| Draggers want to rehash what was settled to everyone else's satisfaction. | "I'm sorry, we've already reached a decision on that." |

And then there are Showoffs. They pretend to be helpful while trying to impress everybody as they spout parliamentary procedure. A staff meeting doesn't need formal debate. Simplify. For example, the "previous question" is a motion meant to put a temporary gag on the talking jag. It's another way of asking everyone if they think there's been enough discussion, and unless two-thirds agree immediately, debate resumes. You can forget the percentage, but move on the intent.

Robbie: "I move the previous question."

Mario: "Thanks, Robbie." (and immediately to the group) "Are you ready to vote on Clark's suggestion?" Or, "We have time to call on two more before we vote."

Come Across as Flexible

Strive for balance in setting the tone and thermostat. A little humor or poking fun at overdone preciseness (not the overly precise people) can relieve tension, but too much and the meeting loses its serious purpose. If you act as though you are one of the gang, you give up control. On the other hand, if you're more strict or formal than necessary, your staff feel they're always on the verge of a verbal lashing.

Apply rules appropriately

Your subordinates are a captive audience. A small staff meeting needs a warmer, more relaxed atmosphere than a large civic association does. You wouldn't use the same parliamentary jargon when presiding in the office that you'd use in the boardroom because that would be unnecessarily stiff and stifling. Even General Robert who wrote the book on parliamentary procedure

(*Rules Of Order*) says rules should fit the needs of the group rather than try to fit the meeting to any rule book.

TIP: Keep everything in proportion while presiding. Watch for undisguised signs—squirming, frowning, scratching heads, talking to each other—that say a subject is exhausted and move along.

Strategy Your objective, as the presider, is to be fair and consistent, giving everyone equal treatment. You can do this without invoking The Rules on which fairness is based.

(1) If you want a matter put to a vote, majority rules after the minority has had its say.

(2) For informal meetings, forget about getting motions made and seconded. Just state (or restate) the issue and ask for discussion. Save formal motions for the record when important policies have to be adopted.

Arnold wanted help with stimulating the flow of ideas at his meetings. Here was a typical exchange that snagged the discussion.

Curtis: "I move to table the question."

Arnold: "Curtis, are you trying to dispose of this matter or just put it aside temporarily?"

Curtis: "I was suggesting we wait to talk about it until we have new information."

Arnold: "Then I believe the motion you want is to postpone to a certain time."

Who cares? Why correct well-meaning Curtis when it's quicker and friendlier to avoid formal voting.

What to say Sense what's needed and apply the Silent Consent rule:

"If nobody objects, let's postpone this until next week when we'll have the data we need for a decision. Any objection?" (Pause. If there is none, go to the next item; if there is an objection, it's no longer silent or unanimous consent and the objector is heard.)

TIP: Beware of the suggestion, "Let's refer this to a committee." It could be a stall to prevent changing the status quo, a means to divert attention from content to procedure. In that case, just back up to the point of disagreement and ask the whole group what it wants to do.

Presiding over a staff meeting is a common sense juggling act—a friendly yet firm application of a few basic rules to guarantee consistency and fair and equal treatment to each member of your team.

How to find out what your group is thinking

Aim for an open, healthful emotional climate for all your meetings. If you're chairing a committee meeting, come prepared to state the purpose and follow up with incisive clusters of questions. For instance,

> "We're here to study and recommend to the executive committee criteria for measuring the success of a project. What are some possible units of measurements that might apply here? What would have to happen for us to consider a project successful?"

At a staff meeting, it can be important to you to hear what your staff thinks before you decide definitely. Save your opinion until the end of the discussion even though you are in charge. Otherwise you'll hear, "Good idea, boss," said in unison. You don't need a bunch of rubber stamps. When you speak first, your staff may feel forced to conform to your norm. A staff meeting can't be democratic. Everyone knows the boss has the last word. Therefore, use phrases that draw out their thinking instead of coloring their views.

> "I know you all feel a part of the company and I can come to you for ideas. The question for our promotion unit is: What's the best approach to increase...?"

"I've listened carefully to your arguments and I
believe we have to do...because..."

Determine if a meeting is needed

If there's no discussion needed, that's not a meeting. It's a lecture. Such procedure is all right to present information quickly
to hundreds of employees, but not for a small group. The same
facts can be furnished cheaper and with less annoyance by other
means—telephone, bulletin board, notices, circulating memos,
newsletter article. No one likes having work interrupted or appointments cancelled just to hear, "I've called you here to read
you the Director's New Executive Order on Parking Spaces."

Sometimes managers legitimately call meetings because they
expect opposition and want to reach their employees before
morale drops. For instance,

> *Manager:* "I want to tell you about an important policy
> change. I think once you understand the background you'll see why...I realize this is a sacrifice
> for everyone of us, but the benefits are...Now, let
> me answer your questions. What concerns you
> the most?"

The manager, putting the needed link in the communication
chain, now can carry upstairs the staff's perception of the move,
along with any hard-to-answer questions.

How to include your staff in the planning

On some policy decisions you really do want to hear staff ideas
on desired results, changing methods, tradeoffs, and so on.

TIP: When your objective is to get good staff ideas, let your
staff "buy into" the plan and become part of the planning.
The guideline is: Ask, don't tell.

Strategy

(1) Face the controversial. Let your staff explore the options
   instead of tabling the item.

(2) Follow a set agenda. Don't skip from one issue to the next without settling each item before you move along.

(3) Alert your staff to the subject matter and otherwise prepare them for discussion.

(4) Make certain that meeting notices arrive early enough to avoid, "I was late for the 9:00 A.M. meeting, my notice arrived at 10 o'clock."

(5) Evaluate the emotional climate and physical arrangements. You'll get more accomplished when the group is comfortable and uncrowded.

To review your methods of meeting preparation and follow-up, go over the Meeting Checklist at the end of the chapter.

Give direction to the person taking minutes

Although a record is important and it keeps the group on track, some people are hesitant to comment if every remark is recorded in the minutes. A crisp, succinct report is also a more useful reference. Here are some do's and don'ts to tell your secretary.

(1) Don't record every word—just the gist.

(2) Get the essence of each report in a few sentences. If it's very important, we'll attach a copy of the report.

(3) Don't summarize debates—only list the decisions.

(4) Don't editorialize—no adjectives for or against.

(5) Write conversationally—no complicated sentences.

(6) Give me a draft of the minutes right after the meeting. Some items will need my immediate attention.

Keep abbreviated minutes by jotting terse notes on your own agenda as each decision is reached. With the combination of written notes and verbal announcements, summarizing results to the group as you finish each item, you'll have good recall afterwards and can prepare your own meeting recap—a follow-up thanking the staff and clearly outlining meeting results and new assignments.

Reach a Decision—Don't Vacillate

With a little practice, you can get issues aired and resolved informally. Your team may start out all fired up, anxious to accomplish your purpose, but find that vacillation burns their energy to ashes. To prevent this, announce a decision after each agenda item even if the decision is to wait for a comparison with figures from next month's report. As the meeting progresses, combine verbal announcements with written notes by each agenda item clarifying who will do what by when. After the meeting, compile a Meeting Summary from your notes which serves as both a record and a follow-up checklist for you and your staff.

How to handle hot potato issues

No matter how well you plan, you have to be prepared for staffers dropping a bombshell during the meeting. Sometimes you can prevent this through required agenda scheduling, but other times the difficulty can't be anticipated.

TIP: Your objective is to resolve any criticism or controversy that pops up unexpectedly. If you bury a problem, it'll come back to haunt you. Or if it's just smoothed over, it isn't settled and will erupt again. If you're too scared to deal with a little annoyance, you won't stand a ghost of a chance with a large problem.

Strategy Plan ahead for the handling of controversial matters at meetings.

(1) Train subordinates to schedule with you new issues for discussion before sounding off at a meeting.
(2) Have a system that allows careful thought and dispatch for dealing with non-scheduled emergency items.

During Andrea's staff meeting, she was caught off guard when Scott brought up the question of changing the schedule of holidays for which employees are given days off. Although the reported rumblings had escalated to an emotional issue, no one was really ready to discuss it.

What To Say Andrea first had to decide if the problem was too important and pressing to postpone. She determined they could wait a week.

> *Andrea:* "Scott, that will be our first issue next week. In the meantime, each of you talk to your people to get a better handle on the problem. . .From now on,

please schedule with my secretary by Tuesday any item you want placed on the agenda for Thursday's meeting. We'll have better discussion with all the data and time needed to reach a conclusion."

Had the issue that was uncovered without warning been too explosive to postpone, Andrea couldn't stop the clock, but she could quickly and effectively give the group time to defuse the bomb by breaking up into small sub-groups for a few minutes, a variation of the 6-6 Plan discussed in the next chapter. You can move decisively by having a plan for dealing with unexpected, controversial matters.

How to expedite amendments to motions

Somehow even simple amendments can turn into a hopeless maze although there are only a few rules to remember:

(1) An amendment must relate the subject being amended.

(2) It's acceptable to change an amendment only once.

(3) If the majority approves the amendment, vote on the proposal as amended.

Here's a less confusing way to handle amendments.

Bonnie: "I propose that the target group be under thirty years old."

Herb: "I'd like to amend Bonnie's proposal, inserting the words 'between twenty-one and' before thirty."

Andrea: "Is that OK with you, Bonnie? How do the rest of you feel about defining the age of the target group as between twenty-one and thirty?"

How to rephrase questions to get better answers

When putting forth questions for group discussion, it's important to zero in on the precise concern. If your questions cover the waterfront, skimming the surface instead of digging down to the basic issue or real problem, all you will get from the group will be scattergun solutions.

> "What do you think would improve our field workers' morale?"

Poor morale isn't the trouble; it's a symptom that trouble exists. Get everyone to concentrate on the real question by going down to the next level. If your goal is to improve morale and productivity, ask:

> "What are some possible causes for the low morale among our field workers? What specifically do they want that they are not now receiving?"

TIP: Sharpen the focus. Your objective is to state the exact problem. In doing so, you are halfway to the desired outcome.

Strategy Ask the questions that enable you to elicit workable answers. It is also important to ask the right question when

(1) *You're not sure what a participant means.* You don't want to appear incompetent in front of your group, but consider that if you don't understand, the others don't either. Ask:

> "Are you saying that...?"
>
> "Would I be correct in interpreting your remark to say...?"
>
> "Please explain how that would work."

(2) *The discussion has become heated.* You tried to break the tension with a joke, then you called a brief recess, but now everybody is still excited. Ask someone you can depend on to set the stage for calmer comments and face-saving solutions.

> "Morey, you're so good at pinpointing issues. Would you please summarize for us both points of view?"

Or ask the group to back track.

> "Let's back up to where there *is* agreement. The fact that such a project *did* succeed two years ago..."

Now, what would you say is the precise point of disagreement?"

You have to ask the basic questions if you want to get feasible
answers.

Rather than rising to every point of order you can run a more
dynamic meeting by sensing a point of "oughta." Let your good
manners and common sense tell you to avoid getting bogged down,
to resolve the issues discussed by your staff, and that it's better
to have a little less decorum than to bore them. Above all, keep in
mind the real reason for meeting—to find out what the group is
thinking, not to bottle up their thoughts.

MEETING CHECKLIST

Planning and Agenda

( ) Who should attend the meeting?

( ) Are these participants (or which participants) are capable of discussing that issue?

( ) Are additional persons, either guests or knowledgeable employees, needed as resource?

( ) Have they been invited?

( ) What agenda items are needed to accomplish the objective?

( ) What is a realistic amount of time to resolve each agenda item?

( ) What data and materials should be attached to the agenda and sent in advance to encourage good participant discussion?

( ) Has the agenda been prepared in the form of a meeting time schedule (time blocks for each item)?

( ) What methods and techniques will be used to present the information and get audience participation?

( ) Has everyone who will take part been contacted, including a discussion of the content and time allocation with those giving reports?

( ) Has the time schedule been adjusted if necessary?

( ) Have arrangements been made for early distribution of the meeting notice (with agenda) to all participants?

( ) Have arrangements been made for the taking of minutes?

Physical Arrangements

( ) If the meeting is to be held in a private office, are there enough chairs to be arranged in a half-circle facing the desk?

( ) If not, has the meeting been scheduled in a convenient place with adequate parking?

( ) Are there good directional signs?

( ) Is the room the appropriate size, figuring no more than 15 people for good discussion or plan to break up into smaller groups?

( )   Is the seating comfortable but not too cozy, with movable chairs?

( )   If needed, can meals or coffee breaks be provided there?

( )   Does the room have whatever special features are required—blackboard, microphones, lectern, stage area, screen and light control for visuals?

( )   Is there good lighting, ventilation, and noise control?

( )   Will everyone have a clear view of the speakers, with no large columns in the way?

( )   Is there room enough for tables, chairs, and planned displays, exhibits, and tables with reference materials?

Meeting Aids and Visual Aids

( )   Is there a sufficient quantity of required supplies—notepads, pencils, name tags, water pitchers and glasses?

( )   Have all required handouts been prepared?

( )   Does the supply box contain scissors, masking and transparent tape, blackboard chalk and eraser, and felt markers?

( )   Will an easel and flip chart be needed?

( )   If planning to use slides, film, video tape, or overhead projector, is the equipment in good condition?

( )   Is a technician available to operate the equipment?

( )   Are there sufficient electrical outlets and extension cords?

( )   Are transparencies or slides in sequence, film or tape rewound and ready to go?

Emotional Climate

( )   Have outgoing, friendly people been assigned as greeters?

( )   If using small sub-groups, have well-prepared discussion leaders and recorders been assigned?

( )   Have opening remarks been prepared to welcome participants, highlight the meeting objective, and encourage everyone to join the discussion?

( )   Have brief, interesting, personalized, and gracious introductions been prepared?

( )   Have bits of continuity been written on the agenda to interject a little good natured humor without needling anyone?

( ) Have gracious, appreciative, and positive closing remarks been prepared, ready to be added to the summary of meeting results?

Post Meeting

( ) Have materials promised to participants at the meeting been sent to them?

( ) Were notes of appreciation sent?

( ) Was a meeting summary prepared and sent to participants?

( ) If follow-up action was indicated, was a who/what/when type of assignment sheet part of the meeting summary, and followed by appropriate check-up phone calls?

( ) If any newsworthy action took place, was a report made to company officials, an article submitted to the company newsletter or a release sent to the media?

( ) Was there an evaluation of the meeting to determine how well it met objectives, and if any changes resulted from the meeting?

( ) Could there be improvement next time in the planning?

CHAPTER 16

$$\big(\qquad\qquad\qquad\big)$$

Extracting Great Ideas from Your Group

QUIZ #16. DO YOU GET GOOD SUGGESTIONS FROM YOUR TEAM?

There's a gold mine of good ideas among your subordinates just waiting to be unearthed. Are you doing all you can to tap into this potential? Evaluate your style by choosing the way you'd ordinarily act or react in the following situations. The interpretation of your choices follows.

1. You have to report back to management your group's recommendation on a proposed revision.

   (a) You urge an immediate, unanimous decision.

   (b) You set a time limit for reaching a unanimous decision.

   (c) It doesn't matter if the decision isn't unanimous.

2. At a meeting when two subordinates start arguing about a procedure, you

   (a) tell them to cool it, everybody should act harmoniously.

   (b) let them and the others resolve the matter.

(c) quickly stop the argument by announcing your decision.

3. The same three staff members always dominate the discussion, but their points are consistently well-taken.

   (a) Since the major points are covered, calling on others would be a boring rehash.
   (b) You appreciate their leadership and say so.
   (c) You ask direct questions of others who may have some contributions.

4. If a member of your team criticizes the operation, you

   (a) accept criticism as a way to improve.
   (b) shift discussion from what's wrong to praising what's good.
   (c) feel wounded by this act of disloyalty.

5. Your team, disecting a project's poor results, focuses on someone's motives for the blunder. You

   (a) are inclined to agree, and say so.
   (b) are inclined to agree, but keep still.
   (c) interrupt, asking that the discussion stick to correcting the issue.

6. In accepting suggestions from your staff, you

   (a) thank them and pat their heads for trying.
   (b) make sure they understand you are in total command.
   (c) promise to consider these carefully.

7. You've read that quality circles produce good suggestions,

   (a) and agree those doing the job are in the best position to offer solutions.
   (b) but feel the process is too difficult to set up.
   (c) but feel management is better trained to find solutions.

8. To get help in solving a pressing problem for your unit, you

   (a) go solely to your boss for alternatives.

(b) call your staff together for suggestions.

(c) you seek input only from your top assistants.

Interpretation

1.   All decisions don't have to be unanimous. There is often merit in a minority report.

2.   Once you say what you want or insist on harmony, few subordinates will disagree or offer other ideas.

3.   By allowing a few to dominate the discussion, you discourage every one else from participating and miss hearing other experiences or points of view that might be valuable.

4.   You control how criticism is given and received. If people aren't free to point out what they think is wrong, you'll never get their ideas for improvement.

5.   Regardless of the validity, personal attacks destroy a group meeting. Moreover, correcting a subordinate should be private. Go back to attacking the problem.

6.   An authoritative leadership style may intimidate subordinates. If you're paternalistic, they may resent your condescending. You don't have to do what they suggest, but if they know you weigh their ideas, they'll keep trying.

7.   If you're looking for new approaches, try some variation of the quality circle. Those doing the actual work often have answers that might otherwise be overlooked.

8.   When there's a problem, it's fine to get help from your boss and your top aides, but why not enlarge your options by also listening to your subordinates?

HOW TO GET YOUR STAFF TO TELL YOU THEIR SUGGESTIONS

While a company without supervisors to make final decisions is heading straight into chaos, there are some decisions that can be apportioned or made jointly. When workers feel that they're part of the group, they want to share in its problems.

Reports show that organizations that were strongest while under stress are those that invite their employees to share in the decisions affecting their work. You can help your subordinates reach these decisions. When they learn to examine facts and resolve issues, they are growing in leadership as well as helping you.

Rubbing their brains together will spark new suggestions. To draw out their thoughts, remember

- Building pride improves productivity
- Eleven problem-solving techniques for capturing their suggestions

Building Pride Improves Productivity

The better product or service exists only because of the people who work for the company or agency. The more they understand the goals, policies, procedures and problems, the more they can help with creative solutions. As standards go up, so does pride in the work, along with greater productivity and cost reduction.

Sharing decisions increases creative thinking

To get your people participating, first examine your own brand of leadership. Check the style which best describes you.

( ) *Authoritarian* You're away a day and ask, "Is the company still here?" Believing yourself indispensable, no one else makes decisions. When you're gone, where does the company stand?

( ) *Paternalistic* You've got your subordinates' problems solved before they're aware they have any. You're there for every single little step. Having the work done right is all that matters. There's small chance for your workers to grow on the job or increase their self-confidence.

( ) *Laissez-Faire* At the other extreme, you go beyond non-interference to indifference. Whatever your workers ask, you'll look into it later. You never do. You're so busy relaxing and enjoying your honor, they've begun to suspect you're totally disinterested in how well (or poorly) your unit is functioning.

( ) *Participatory* This is as close as you can get to democratic and still maintain control. "I want to hear what you think about this" are the sweetest words to a subordinate's ears. When your workers have a sense of belonging and truly feel a part of the company, they want to share in its problems. Employee participation may be your most potent tool to improve pride and productivity and to reduce bickering.

Creating a healthful emotional climate encourages participation

Sharing in the solutions, however, is only possible when a boss allows subordinates to participate. If you receive all criticism as treason, the emotional climate is sticky and damp. Let some fresh ideas flow and stop worrying about disrupting the status quo.

TIP: Encourage your team to discuss controversial issues. This helps participants develop personally and your unit move productively. If everyone always agrees on everything, you are putting too much stress on harmony, an extremely weak base from which to progress.

Strategy   Your objective is to raise the level of discussion.

(1) Assure reciprocal respect and concentration on getting answers.
(2) Give subordinates the opportunity to express dissatisfaction with the current status. That's a first step to thinking about potential ways to do it better, faster, or cheaper.

Time after time Emmy finished a staff meeting drained and discouraged because her group couldn't reach unanimous decisions. It's those strong individualists who cause the lack of unity, she complained. She tried to stop all criticism because she resented the disrespectful manner in which it was leveled.

What to say   Part of the art of presiding is knowing when to break in and tactfully correct anyone who's going off base.

Wes: "Sean is slowing down the operation by—"

Emmy: "Wes, are you saying we need a better system to speed up the operation?"

One of the best ways to maintain the climate that encourages constructive criticism and creative thought is by insisting on respect for everyone present. You simply don't allow personal insults by redirecting the criticism to the issue.

Helping group members to play valuable roles

Each member of a group plays a different role—whatever suits his or her capabilities and personality. If you help your staff understand their individual contributions, then their self-worth will expand along with their usefulness. Spot a potential that a subordinate has for doing something well and communicate this ("I really admire the way you make everyone in the room feel comfortable about speaking out") and that person will knock himself out to live up to your high regard.

People sometimes don't realize how valuable they are to your unit or company unless you spell out how they help. You can identify most of your staff from this list of constructive roles that members play in a group. Some play more than one. Encourage your subordinates by letting them know you appreciate their assistance.

1. **Information Seekers** Lack facts and feel it's their task to ask. The information falls also upon the ears of those too shy or proud to question.

2. **Opinion Seekers** Detectives seeking perspectives, they want to know why we weigh certain values above others.

3. **Opinion Givers** They point up possibilities others might not foresee and, when they state their beliefs, others may not agree.

4. **Elaborators** Their example is ample to draw a clear picture of the meaning or outcome. They tactfully take another's point and give it depth.

5. **Coordinators** They pull together the pieces so that various ideas and suggestions fit the company's activities.

6. **Orienters** They put the discussion back on track and keep the goal in front of the group.

7. **Technicians** Whatever they do (rearrange chairs, pass out pads, and so on) they quickly and graciously add to the smooth flow of the meeting.

8. **Recorders** They imprint suggestions—on paper or in their minds—and remind others of main points already made.

9. **Initiaters** Bundles of energy. Their let's-get-going-on-this-right-now attitude stimulates action. Always an approach to get you started.

10. **Testers** They want to be sure it's tactical and practical before you decide definitely.

11. **Diagnosticians** Stripping away mere symptoms, they get the core to the floor. They analyze and localize the basic problem.

12. **Evaluators** They show the next step when you're snagged on the pro and con. They state the group's feelings when they summarize and appraise.

13. **Standard Setters** They feel and reveal high ideals. They deserve acclaim after they uplift your aim.

14. **Encouragers** Their understanding, acceptance, and praise make others want to contribute.

15. **Gate Keepers** They help the silent speak up by asking direct questions or proposing a time limit to debate.

16. **Group Testers** They express a view, not necessarily their own, but guaranteed to get others talking. Their action gets reaction out in the open.

17. **Harmonizers** They mediate tiffs by narrowing differences. They relieve the gaff with a laugh and substitute reasonableness for cold reason.

18. **Compromisers** They know when to give in a little. Having their own way is not as important as helping the group reach a decision.

Eleven Problem-Solving Techniques for Capturing Suggestions

Actually the term "creative alternatives" connotes a better emphasis than "problem solving." You don't bring your group together to talk about what's wrong but to figure out how to achieve what's right for the group. Besides meeting discussions and employee suggestion awards, the following ways pay off in stimulating thought and in capturing ideas, suggestions and solutions from employees.

TIP: Your objective is to work out a definite answer or plan. Leave sketchy abstractions to the artists. Your group may produce a completely different solution from those first advocated, which is fine. They may come up with something even better—a synthesis, an original product that the whole group created.

---

1. *Problem Census* When the air is filled with general dissatisfaction (as compared to mixed feelings over a particular issue) you can't begin to improve until you can sort things out and state precisely how certain conditions are affecting your group. Take a census. Ask a technician-type participant to assist you.

> "OK, gang, start calling out the problems that most concern you. And I'm asking Gerry to write each suggestion on the blackboard for all of us to see. Don't try to judge or classify. For now, we'll just list your concerns."

This procedure keeps everyone together as they observe the recording and watch the progress. The group then suggests logical divisions of the list and determines which concerns get top priority. The next step is to restate each concern as a positive objective:

From: "The concern is an increasingly high number of turnovers."

To: "The objective is to design a plan that will reduce turnovers by 20 percent in the next year."

The hardest part is figuring out what you want to do. Once you have a clear objective, it's relatively easy to come up with a plan to achieve it.

2. *Brainstorming* What's a trouble spot to Nettie may be unnoticed by Freddy who won't be bothered until there's a blow up. Recognize the sparks early before everyone is inflamed. Brainstorm in small peer groups of eight or less. First, carefully define the issues, one at a time, by asking questions. Put the suggestions on the blackboard until you can agree on the *real* issue.

> "It seems we're not actually concerned with how to get more security guards, but with how to prevent assaults in the parking lot. Do we agree about that?"

Once the question is crystal clear, list all the facts. But bear in mind that assumptions aren't certainties. Don't state what you *think* is so as what you know. Now record every potential solution.

> **TIP:** Initially, you're after quantity, not quality. Get out as many thoughts as possible on how the problem might be solved. It's often the farfetched that ignites the feasible.

One person builds on another's idea, so don't allow any judgmental calls during this part.

> "It'll never work, boss. It's wild."
>
> "It doesn't matter. Right now we're collecting every possible way to deal with the issue."

Next, the group establishes criteria for judging the value of the ideas. You might hear:

Ellen: "I think we need to know whether it would make the problem better or worse."

Alvin: "We have to consider the benefits and if they are worth the cost."

Shirley: "We have a time problem. Whatever we decide, it has to be done within three months."

Then, lead the group into examining every possibility by probability.

> "Based on the considerations just stated, if we do this...How will it affect...?"

Continue the same way for each suggestion until you're ready to put to the test what appears to be the best alternative.

3. *Buzz Sessions* Before dividing into small groups, each to tackle a different problem, a different aspect of the same problem, or the same problem, put the issue into focus with a talk, panel, film or dramatization. Ask one member of each group to act as a discussion leader (DL). Explain the role.

> "1. Your job is to keep the talk on target. Come prepared with pertinent facts and stimulating questions to help the group pool its ideas. Intervene if they go off on a tangent."

> "2. Tactfully cut short the repetitious by setting a time limit to give each one a chance to talk."

> "3. How deeply you delve depends on the group's background. Ask questions the members can relate to, such as 'What works for you when a worker is insubordinate?' "

Another member of each group acts as a recorder to compile the various suggestions and opinions given. Recorders from each group later give summary reports to the entire congregation.

4. *Working Lunch* Place a card on each table indicating the topic to be discussed there. Participants move about the room to see the menu of issues and make their selection by sitting beside their preferred subject. Pre-assign a DL and a recorder for each table.

5. *Six-Six Plan* When you're in the middle of a muddle, huddle. This is good to use at a meeting when an unexpected, controversial problem pops up without warning and you need an instant answer. Start by saying:

> "OK, team, let's resolve this quickly. Divide yourselves into groups of six for six minutes." (The plan is pliant—five or seven might be a better number for you.) "Turn to your immediate neighbors, clustering your chairs in circles. Each group select a spokesperson to report to the whole meeting."

Should further study be needed, a committee can lead you out of the labyrinth.

6. *Listening Groups* This method sets the stage to hear a variety of viewpoints because parts of the group hear the issue from different angles. Before a talk, film, or video tape, divide into groups with each given a specific question to discuss after the presentation. For example, right before showing a video tape that gives an overview of the company, you might say:

> "Group I, pay particular attention to how you think new employees would react to this at orientation. Group II, think about the suitability of this tape as part of the presentation to potential clients. Group

III, decide if any segments of the video can be used on TV for educating the general public."

7. *Role Playing*   The play's still the thing, but with a spontaneous ring. To get it going, say for instance,

> "We need a couple of volunteers to stage a little unrehearsed dramatization. . .Thanks, Marla and Glen. You two are going to act out a problem we've been hassling with—what to say to the customer who stalls right before signing. The rest of you observe, then offer comments and suggestions for better solutions."

Role playing encourages participation and leads to a deeper understanding among your workers as to why some of them haven't been as effective as they'd hoped. The cures come in palatable doses. The lessons are retained longer because they're enjoyable. A word of caution, though. No fair commenting on the talent of your would-be thespians.

8. *Unsigned Questionnaire*   Employees who sign their names to a questionnaire often reply the way they think the boss wants them to. Because it gives the freedom to be truthful, the unsigned questionnaire can be more useful than those requiring identification. Be careful to word your question so that it gives you the *exact* information you are seeking. This exercise can help your workers think through problems, often unmasking its core, revealing attitudes not anticipated, or ideas that would otherwise never have occurred to them. To facilitate compiling, the question often takes this form:

> *Q:*   "To what extent did the subject matter in the training course meet your needs? Rate on a scale of 1 to 5, with 1 being very little and 5 very much."
>
> *A:*   "(1)—(2)—(3)—(4)—(5)—"

9. *Morale Survey*   When spirits seem to be dragging and you're not sure why, this will help you get a handle on the undercurrent. To find out if the dissatisfaction is widespread or confined, list all the complaints that have been circulating. By each complaint, the employee can check his/her choice:

( ) I agree strongly
( ) I agree
( ) I don't know
( ) I disagree
( ) I strongly disagree

On the bottom, have a section where workers can write what's really bugging them.

> *Comments:* "Please elaborate on any of the above items or add any we've left out."

10. *Gallup Poll* To help you understand employee attitudes, counteract complaints or make decisions on which way to go, query a cross-section, a random sampling of all your subordinates, asking each one to respond to the same question with multiple-choice replies. For example:

Q: "In your opinion, how effective is the new procedure recently initiated on inventory control?"

A: ( ) very effective
( ) somewhat effective
( ) no difference
( ) somewhat ineffective
( ) very ineffective

Report replies in percentages. Follow with your analysis and then invite discussion.

11. *Quality Circles* Nobody knows the job better than the one doing it. Quality circles are increasingly popular as a way to get employee participation. When approached properly, experience has shown that valuable knowledge can be extracted from the group. The company gets an improved product or service, and the employee gets greater pride and a happier environment.

To obtain this information, train workers in the techniques they need—brainstorming, data collection, decision analysis, and speaking/visual presentations. Small circles, groups of eight to ten employed in the same kind of job, meet voluntarily about an hour a week. This is an on-going process to identify, select and analyze applicable problems.

Here's an example of an award-winning recommendation from a quality circle in a suburban police district.

> "We recommend purchasing equipment that would enable us to realign our police cars in our district garage instead of transporting the vehicles back and forth to the central downtown facility."

The top brass agreed, and this resulted in a considerable annual saving as well as a substantial decrease in vehicle downtime.

For circle members, the big moment comes when, showing their collective talents, they deliver to management a presentation describing the problem and their recommended solution. After a review, management decides whether or not to implement. Whichever way, the workers know that the head honchos have *really* listened to them.

* * *

Griping is good only as a first step in coming to grips with a difficult situation. It can help you see where you want to be. Once the question becomes clear, let your subordinates share in some of the decisions that affect their work. If they're part of the planning, they'll be there for the problems and the new creative solutions.

Summary

MAKE YOURSELF MORE SALEABLE
IN THE MARKETPLACE

Even if you were the world's greatest contortionist, you couldn't see yourself as others do or hear the way you sound. So you have to "get outside of yourself" as though you were listening to someone else to recognize how you are coming across. What must you do to improve the potential you already possess?

1. *Force yourself to think before you speak.* Determine the outcome you desire. Then you can express logical action, not emotional reaction. When you hear yourself using strategic, workable words, the job becomes more fun. And since you spend at least a third of your day at the office, that's a mighty important consideration.

2. *If you can't find the circumstances you want, create them.* By now you've discovered that you can't change the people you think may be holding you back. But you can change the way you think about them, act toward them and talk to them. You can make things happen for you.

3. *Listen carefully and speak clearly, confidently, and fearlessly.* This lets you cash in on your initiative and enthusiasm—a combination top executives look for. You can improve their perception of you just by donning antennae to pick up on what's important to your company, department, boss, colleagues, and subordinates. Focus on the real problem. Get others excited about your proposals. Modestly toot your own horn and get others to toot it for you.

Speaking well in daily combat impresses decision-makers who hear you as a potential leader. You impress your colleagues who get the message that your star is rising and jump on your bandwagon. You also impress your subordinates who become loyal followers and productive workers. The ability to communicate is a skill that will tip the scales in your favor at the office. It will also spill over to enrich your personal life.

THE TEN MOST IMPORTANT RULES TO REMEMBER

These ten rules can help you the most in getting across to the people you work with.

1. *Say What You Must To Make Friends, Mend Fences, And Eliminate Enemies.* You never know whom you'll need to help you get where you want to go. Gossiping and knocking others will come back to haunt you. Instead, cultivate additional friendships which require *being* a friend as well.

2. *Express Sensitivity By Letting Others Save Their Dignity.* Don't tell people they're wrong or back them into a corner. Criticize tactfully and constructively, with the obvious aim to improve the situation, not to cut someone down to size.

3. *Keep A Civil Tongue And Treat Everyone The Same—Politely.* Don't use one manner for the boss and another for subordinates. Declare real appreciation to anyone who assists you. Remember, you are more effective delivering a devastating remark in a slow, low, controlled voice.

4. *Talk About The Other Person's Concerns.* Ask about topics they're involved in. Develop the "You" attitude, seeing situations through the other guy's eyes to effectively sell, persuade, negotiate or discuss.

5. *Use Body Language To Convey Your Interest In Others.* Whether you're part of a discussion, giving a speech or just listening, maintain constant eye contact. React with a smile, nod or head shake. Avoid impatient gestures and nervous moves.

6. *Assert Your Opinions And Suggestions Without Being Aggressive.* It is obnoxious to dogmatically cram your views down someone's throat. Instead, plan ahead what you are going to say and, when appropriate, visually dramatize or showcase your ideas.

7. *Admit It When You've Blundered.* People understand this and can forgive you. But if you wait too long to say you're sorry, the situation will fester and be much harder to correct.

8. *Ask For Ideas From The People Doing The Work.* You can't plan in a vacuum. You need to know the thoughts of those in the best position to make it better, faster or cheaper.

9. *Communicate The Benefits From Whatever You Want Done.* Make others feel good about doing work for you. Don't ask that they do a personal favor to you, but rather that they do a personal favor to themselves because the proposed action is important to them.

10. *Request Help And Advice* People love to lend a hand and give their two cents. It makes them feel important. Tap into the experiences of others. You're not supposed to know everything, but you are expected to keep learning.

Index

A

B